MUSIC BY

EDITORS

HEINZ VON FOERSTER

Professor of Biophysics
and of Electrical Engineering
University of Illinois
Urbana

JAMES W. BEAUCHAMP

Assistant Professor of Electrical Engineering
University of Illinois
Urbana

John Wiley and Sons, Inc.

COMPUTERS

AUTHORS

JAMES W. BEAUCHAMP

HERBERT BRÜN

M. DAVID FREEDMAN

LEJAREN HILLER

M. V. MATHEWS

J. R. PIERCE

J. K. RANDALL

ARTHUR ROBERTS

L. ROSLER

GERALD STRANG

HEINZ VON FOERSTER

New York · London · Sydney · Toronto

Library of Congress Catalog Card Number: 69-19244
SBN 471 91030 9
Printed in the United States of America

The Authors

JAMES W. BEAUCHAMP, Ph.D.

Assistant Professor of Electrical Engineering
Department of Electrical Engineering
University of Illinois, Urbana, Illinois

HERBERT BRÜN, B.A., M.A.

Assistant Professor of Music
School of Music
University of Illinois, Urbana, Illinois

M. DAVID FREEDMAN, Ph.D.

Bendix Research Laboratories
Southfield, Michigan

LEJAREN A. HILLER, Ph.D.

Professor of Music
School of Music
University of Illinois, Urbana, Illinois

MAX V. MATHEWS, Ph.D.

Bell Telephone Laboratories
Murray Hill, New Jersey

JOHN R. PIERCE, Ph.D.

Bell Telephone Laboratories
Murray Hill, New Jersey

J. K. RANDALL, Ph.D.

Professor of Music
Department of Music
Woolworth Center of Musical Studies
Princeton University
Princeton, New Jersey

ARTHUR ROBERTS, Ph.D.

Department of High Energy Physics
Argonne National Laboratory
Argonne, Illinois

L. ROSLER, Ph.D.

Bell Telephone Laboratories
Murray Hill, New Jersey

GERALD STRANG, Ph.D.

Chairman, Department of Music
California State College at Long Beach
Long Beach, California

HEINZ VON FOERSTER, Ph.D.

Professor of Biophysics and of
Electrical Engineering
Department of Electrical Engineering
University of Illinois, Urbana, Illinois

To Rowena Swanson

Whoever is fearful and afraid,
let him return and depart.

JUDG. 8: 7.3

Foreword

Since the electronic computer was invented, its usefulness to society has been limited more by the imagination of man than by the capability of the hardware. The possibility of a computer creating music, art, or literature is perhaps obscure only because our pride forces us to believe these areas are man's exclusive provinces.

At the 1966 Fall Joint Computer Conference, Professor Heinz Von Foerster organized a highly creative, imaginative and enjoyable session on "Computers in Music." The papers presented at the session were received with great enthusiasm; and form the basis of this book. The ideas advanced here may well lead to exciting and publicly accepted music of the future.

Dr. William H. Davidow
Technical Program Chairman
1966 Fall Joint Computer Conference

Preface

This book owes its existence to a series of lucky circumstances. When in spring of 1966 the "Call for Papers" for the Fall Joint Computer Conference to be held in San Francisco reached computer-minded members at our university, it was David Freedman, then at the Biological Computer Laboratory, with his mind on computation and his ears on checking the quality of computer-generated sounds (1) (2) (3), who immediately suggested organizing a whole session on the applications of computers in music.

Freedman's enthusiasm was contagious, and in no time enough speakers easily to enliven two sessions were ready to come with their manuscripts, films, and tapes to enact, so to say, the computerized "Meistersinger" of San Francisco. Technically, this presented no small problem, for precision tape-recording and playback equipment had to be set up; movie projectors, lantern slides of various dimensions and other audio-visual aids were needed, and, on top, the personnel had to be found to operate all these contraptions flawlessly.

Luckily again, the organization of this conference was in the hands of very able young men, Dr. George Glaser of McKinsey and Company, who was chairman of the conference, and Dr. William H. Davidow of Hewlett-Packard, who organized the whole program. There temperaments were perfectly matched to the spirit of this session. This was not only borne out by the fact that, at the last minute, this session was given prime time and a prominent space in the conference; nevertheless all the equipment that was needed was operable and professionally operated. Also they avoided a major crisis that arose when the operators wanted to walk out on the session when it ran overtime. Unnoticed by the large audience, new contracts were negotiated and signed with the unions while the show went on smoothly.

When, after three hours, the show was over, the performers were tired but happy; the program appeared to have been in balance and the various viewpoints to have complemented each other. The musical examples helped make the points. The audience was tired too, but the responses had a larger spectrum. Although the computer and systems people were stimulated and amused, most of the curious were still puzzled and the music critics seemed definitely to be depressed. Howard Taubman of *The New York Times* was clearly pessimistic: "As for musicians, they obviously have plenty to worry over—not in the reproduction by the computer of instrumental sounds like those of a violin or horn, which the machine can do after a fashion but which the musician can manage much better. But the day is approaching when a composer can freely bypass the living performer. Oh, brave new world for composers! But what, alas, will be the fate of interpreters?" (4).

Evoking George Crabbe's theorem: "Habit with him was all the test of truth; 'It must be right: I've done it from my youth'" we argued that we may succeed in getting our points across if that which was said could be read and that which was played only once could be heard again at one's leisure and—hopefully—pleasure. Thus the idea for this book was born. Soon afterwards letters of invitation to all participants went out, and even the busiest of authors could not resist responding to communications initiated by a graphical command "READ" (Figure 1).

Soon after the first manuscripts and tapes had arrived, it happened—luckily—that Mr. Cletus M. Wiley of John Wiley & Sons, Inc., Publishers, stepped into the office of one of us, only to ask whether there was something new worthwhile to be published. We mentioned the contemplated book, and the unusual format, which not only discusses but also plays music by computers, stimulated his enterprising mind. The realization of the book was initiated.

An ordered mind desires to have a subject matter presented in an orderly fashion. This asks for some taxonomy, that is, the method of finding classes into which some given objects can be put. This is not only a more difficult problem than that of distributing objects into some given classes, but also an ambiguous one with many possible solutions, as one San Francisco sea food restauranteur had to conclude after he boasted "We serve everything that swims!": One patron asked for Esther Williams.

While editing this book we faced a similar difficulty: choosing the major topics that would best reflect the aim and content of the articles listed under them. Because "best" is in this case a highly subjective judgment, we are aware that the rationale for the choice of the following three topics can be argued:

   I. Systems and Programs.

   II. Algorithms in Composition.

   III. Aesthetics.

The choice listed above may be defended by pointing out the learned discussions of the necessary organization of computer systems to

Figure 1.   An (audio)-visual device for facilitating the reading response in busy authors.

generate controlled sounds and of the structure of programs for computer generated music presented in the articles and examples by Freedman, Beauchamp, and Roberts, which are listed under "Systems and Programs."

Hiller and Mathews and Rosler seem particularly interested in exploring compositional techniques by using formal or graphical algorithms. Consequently, their contributions appear under the general heading of "Algorithms in Composition."

The crucial question of the *significance* of computer generated music appears to be foremost in the minds of the authors Brün, Pierce and Mathews, Randall, and Strang who speak of "desires," "dissonances," "imperfections," "tantalizations," and other anthropomorphic concepts that require judgments on what has been perceived. Following Aristotle, who considered aesthetics (derived from the Greek for perception) to be the theory of those cognitive processes in which judgment enters perception, we classified the articles and examples of these authors under "Aesthetics." We are aware of the horror this terminology may cause some readers, and perhaps rightly so, for this perfectly good term has been abused time and again. However we feel that a clean concept will always come out clean when properly used.

It is now upon us to express our gratitude to all those who contributed their time and effort in making this publication possible; the authors who cooperated splendidly in getting their manuscripts, illustrations, and tapes finished on time; the Directorate of Information Sciences of the Air Force Office of Scientific Research for its unswerving moral support; the editorial and clerical staff of the Biological Computer Laboratory of our University, particularly Mrs. Patricia Smith, Mrs. Jane Spears, Mrs. Alexis Peterson, and Miss Janet Ficken who tirelessly checked and rechecked the consistency of this kaleidoscopic manuscript and typed and retyped various opaque sections until their meaning became transparent. Last, but not least, we admire the courage and taste of the publisher, and particularly the patience of Mr. George V. Novotny, who produced this unusual volume.

However, should there remain errors in exposition or presentation, it is we who must take the blame and not those who so generously helped in bringing music by computers to a wider audience.

H. V. F.
J. W. B.

Urbana, Illinois

REFERENCES

[1] M. D. Freedman, *A Technique for the Analysis of Musical Instrument Tones,* Tech. Report No. 6 (10718), University of Illinois, Urbana (1965).

[2] M. D. Freedman, A Digital Computer for the Electronic Music Studio, *J. Aud. Eng. Soc.,* **15**, 43–50 (1967).

[3] M. D. Freedman, Analysis of Musical Instrument Tones, *J. Acoust. Soc. Am.,* **41**, 793–806 (1967).

[4] H. Taubman, "Play It Again, I.B.M.," *The New York Times* (November 14, 1966).

CONTENTS

INTRODUCTION

HEINZ VON FOERSTER
Sounds and Music   3

I.   PROGRAMS AND SYSTEMS

M. DAVID FREEDMAN
On-line Generation of Sound   13

JAMES W. BEAUCHAMP
A Computer System for Time-Variant Harmonic
Analysis and Synthesis of Musical Tones   19

ARTHUR ROBERTS
Some New Developments in Computer-generated Music   63

II.   ALGORITHMS IN COMPOSITION

LEJAREN HILLER
Some Compositional Techniques Involving the
Use of Computers   71

M. V. MATHEWS and L. ROSLER
Graphical Language for the Scores of Computer-
generated Sounds   84

III.   AESTHETICS

HERBERT BRÜN
Infraudibles   117

J. K. RANDALL
Operations on Wave Forms   122

J. R. PIERCE and M. V. MATHEWS
Control of Consonance and Dissonance with
Nonharmonic Overtones   129

GERALD STRANG
The Problem of Imperfection in Computer Music   133

Introduction

Mathematics is music for the mind;
Music is mathematics for the soul.

ANONYMOUS

Sounds and Music

HEINZ VON FOERSTER

University of Illinois
Urbana, Illinois

Biologically speaking, all auditory systems serve primarily one and only one purpose: to infer from the sounds that are perceived the sources that produced these sounds. When these sources are identified, more clues relating to the state and kind of its environment are available to an organism, and in a few tenths of a second it may swing from a state of utter tranquility into one of a dozen or two modes of behavior: attack, fight, mate, eat, and so on, depending on what is implied by the presence of a particular source. The first step in economizing the enormous task of mapping an almost indefinite variety of signals into a few modes of behavior given to the perceptive and cognitive apparatus of an organism is to classify the sources so that it may identify the "roar of a lion," hence a "lion," or the "hiss of a viper," hence a "viper."

Mathematically speaking, this task amounts to a computation of invariants in a set of sources under various transformations, or, putting it differently, to establishing what is common in all lions that we may identify them as one of a kind or in all vipers that we know them to be different from lions, representing a class in themselves. Visually, such transformations are usually topological, that is, transformations in shape in which neighborhoods are preserved. A viper may curl into various forms and still be recognized as a viper unless neighborhoods are severed; the viper is cut into pieces. This essential change of its topological structure has important consequences; the pieces are no longer considered to be harmful.

Acoustically, these transformations are usually of scaling, that is, changes in size made by maintaining the essential structure of the sound source.

There are two questions that have to be answered if we wish to comprehend the processes that permit an organism to infer the source of a

3

sound by perceiving the sound. First we may ask: What remains invariant in the signal when the source is enlarged or diminished in size? This is answered by relying on our understanding of the physics of sounds or the field of acoustics. Second, we may ask: How does a nervous system compute these invariants? This is answered by relying on our understanding of the structure and function of neural networks or in the field of neurophysiology.

Let us consider the physics first. Imagine two "musical instruments," as in Figure 1, which consist of strings and bells in resonant cavities of like shape but of different size, the linear dimension of the larger instrument being k times that of the smaller. We now excite, say, the large device and generate a sound with a spectrum of fundamentals

$$F_0, F_1, F_2, F_3, \ldots, F_i, \ldots$$

and all their harmonics

$$F_0, 2F_0, 3F_0, \ldots, jF_0, \ldots$$
$$F_1, 2F_1, 3F_1, \ldots, jF_1, \ldots$$
$$F_1, 2F_1, 3F_i, \ldots, jF_i, \ldots,$$

with i and j representing all integers $0 \rightarrow \infty$.

Similarly, if we now excite the small device, we have the fundamentals

$$f_0, f_1, f_2, f_3, \ldots, f_i, \ldots$$

and all their harmonics

$$f_0, 2f_0, 3f_0, \ldots, jf_0, \ldots$$
$$f_1, 2f_1, 3f_1, \ldots, fj_0, \ldots$$
$$f_i, 2f_i, 3f_i, \ldots, jf_i, \ldots,$$

again with i and j representing all integers from $0 \rightarrow \infty$.

We know that the fundamental frequencies f_i of the small device will be just k times the fundamental frequencies of the large device

$$f_i = kF_i.$$

This makes the ratio of any pair of fundamental frequencies F_a and F_b (a and b standing for any particular values of i) not only an invariant within the harmonic spectrum of a particular size of this device

$$\frac{F_a}{F_b} = \frac{jF_a}{jF_b}.$$

because of the cancellation of the like multiplier j in the right-hand

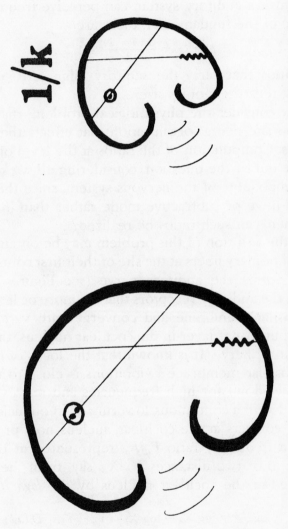

Figure 1. Two acoustical devices of like shape and construction but of different size, the large one generated from the small one by applying a "scaling factor" *k*.

5

side of this equality, but also an invariant for any such device, regardless of its size:

$$\frac{f_a}{f_b} = \frac{kF_a}{kF_b} = \frac{F_a}{F_b},$$

because of the cancellation of the like multiplier, the "scaling factor," in the middle term of the series of the equalities above.

If an organism's auditory system can perceive frequencies up to the nth harmonic of the fundamental, there are

$$N = \binom{n}{2} = \frac{n\,(n-1)}{2} \simeq 1/2\ n^2$$

frequency ratios that carry the auditory "signature" of the source of these sounds, regardless of its size.

Let us now consider the physiological problem; that is the question of the appropriate neural organization that effects the computation of the invariants. Computation of the ratios at the level of a single neuron appears to be out of the question, considering all we know of these remarkable components of the nervous system, since they seem to function in an additive or subtractive mode rather than in a multiplicative one. How, then, can such ratios be realized?

A clue to the solution of this problem may be obtained if we inspect the spacing of primary fibers at the site of their first contact with the fiber bundle that forms the auditory nerve (see Figure 2). These fibers emerge from the auditory receptors that are more or less equally spaced along the basilar membrane and converge with various densities on the first computational layer in the cochlear nucleus, the site of contact with the auditory nerve. It is known that the locus of maximum amplitude of the basilar membrane's vibrations is close to the basal region (at the oval window) for high frequencies and moves steadily toward the apical end with a continuous lowering of frequencies. The variation in density of contacts at the cochlear nucleus now proceeds in such a fashion that a frequency ratio F_a/F_b, represented at the basilar membrane as a ratio of two distances X_a/X_b, say, from the apical end, will be represented at the cochlear nucleus by the *logarithm* of this ratio

$$\log\frac{X_a}{X_b} = \log X_a - \log X_b = Y_a - Y_b = D\,(a,b)$$

or, equivalently, by the *distance* D between two points, a, b along the cochlear nucleus, each point representing the logarithm of a frequency that has brought the basilar membrane to vibration. Consequently, a constant ratio of frequencies, irrespective of their absolute pitch, will be represented by an invariant interval of length between two excited points along the cochlear nucleus, irrespective of the location of this interval.

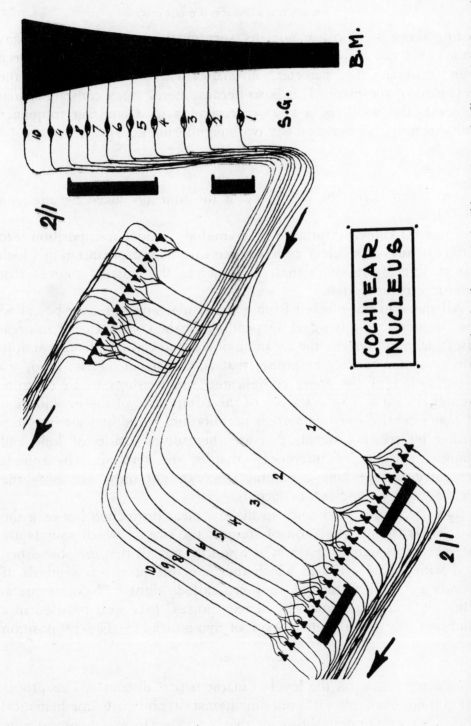

Figure 2.   Mapping of the fibers emerging from the basilar membrane (BM) (basal end top; apical end bottom) onto the fibers originating at the cochlear nucleus. A frequency ratio of one octave (2:1) represented at the basilar membrane by different spatial intervals depending on the frequencies of this ratio, will be mapped into the cochlear nucleus with equal spatial intervals, independent of their location.

The "signature" of a set of sources that differ only in size appears at this level of neural abstractions as a series of excited points (x) separated by fixed intervals

$$\cdots o o x o o o x o o x o o o o x o o \cdots$$

strung along the cochlear nucleus, very much in the same way as any chord—say the major chord of each key—played on a well-tempered piano maintains its "character," no matter where it is struck along the keyboard of the piano. This is so because here, too, a constant spatial interval—the width of a key—corresponds to a constant frequency ratio, namely that between any two neighboring keys

$$\frac{f_{i+1}}{f_i} = \sqrt[12]{2} \simeq 1.0594 \ldots,$$

where f_i stands for the frequency of the tone produced by engaging the ith key.

The well-known invariance of a "melody" under transposition into different keys is a direct consequence of a neural organization which has to infer from the signals it perceives the class of sources that produced these signals.

All that can be inferred from a signal may appropriately be called the "meaning" of this signal. Depending on the complexity of an organism's nervous system, the meaning of a signal can vary from a simple initiation of a feeding response, that is, the signal means "food," to a realization of the most complicated relationships in an environmental situation. The grandeur of the complexity of the organization of man's central nervous system permits him to go at least one step farther by creating signals that are themselves results of long and ramified cascades of inferences—that is, the symbols. The sounds generated by speaking a natural language not only give away the speaker but are vehicles for concepts.

It is of crucial importance to make a clear distinction between the two levels of interpretation of sounds: the one in which sounds are interpreted as signals that hint at a source and all that may be associated with it, the other in which they are interpreted as symbols. If sounds are uninterpretable, they are called "noise." "Noninterpretability" is a concept however; hence "noises" may well be used in a symbolic way on a higher level of symbolization. The proposition

$$2 + 2 = \text{green}$$

is uninterpretable on the level of mathematical discourse. This proposition is not even false; it is pure mathematical nonsense, "mathematical noise." We cannot deny, however, that by its very form of nonsensicality this proposition generates a specific frustration in the search for its meaning, which is precisely the meaning it carries with it.

At this point of the discussion it may have become sufficiently clear that the search for the necessary and sufficient conditions under which sounds will be interpreted as "music" is doomed to fail. This failure is, by all means, not due to a semantic opacity of the term "music." The search is doomed by an intrinsic property of cognitive processes which permit the operators of conceptualizations to become concepts themselves.

Let us consider the sounds that are stored on the records attached to this book. Are these sounds music?

A century ago this question would have been unanimously answered in the negative. Today, however, we have to be more cautious. Why is it that a sizable number of people are willing to pay admission to a concert that to an audience of two generations ago would have constituted cacophony rather than euphony?

The causes for this change in attitude are easily understood if we take a brief glance at the trends in the evolution of Western music, beginning with Pythagoras and terminating—open-ended—with the theories and experiments of those gentlemen who have so kindly consented to present their ideas and results in the form of articles and examples in this book. What are these trends?

They are most clearly understood in information-theoretical terms, namely, as a gradual reduction in the redundancy in works of music or, expressed differently, as a continuous increase in the complexity of sound and composition, hence an increase in the amount of auditory information transmitted during a given interval of time. Redundancy reduction has been achieved over the last two millennia by a steady abolishment of constraints on three levels: specificity of waveforms (sounds), selection of frequencies (scales), and rules of synchronism and succession (composition).

With the invention of new musical instruments down through the centuries and their integration into an orchestra which originally consisted only of lyre and flute, musical sound acquired, by the beginning of our century the grandiose richness, depth, and variety of dimensions unthinkable a thousand or two thousand years ago. The Pythagorean seven-tone scale based on "pure" frequency intervals with ratios of $2/1$, $3/2$, and $5/4$ (corresponding, of course, to the second, third, and fifth harmonics) was found to be an "open" tonal system; that is, ever-new frequencies are generated if a tone, other than the fundamental, is taken as the start of a Pythagorean scale in another key. Consequently, it was replaced in the seventeenth century by the "well-tempered" scale of equal intervals each with a ratio of $\sqrt[12]{2}/1$, which for the first time offered musicians a "closed" tonal system, the 12-tone scale.

With this new scale, transition from key to key may be smoothly accomplished; the earlier constraints on harmony and melody have been abolished. Wagner, Richard Strauss, and Stravinsky made full use of this possibility, but it was Hauer and Schönberg who recognized the crucial features of the well-tempered 12-tone scale, namely, the equivalence of tones within a chord and the invariance of ratios against translation in pitch. With this observation, they opened new possibilities for the composer and further removed constraints regarding synchronism and succession.

It is possible to push these generalizations even further? The answer is clearly "Yes." We may challenge the validity of constraints in sound by a given set of musical instruments; we may challenge the validity of the constraints given by a scale that divides the octave into precisely 12 intervals. The number 12 has nothing to offer to make it preferred over any other number, except that the 12-tone scale happens to provide good approximations for the Pythagorean intervals of 3/2 and 5/4. However, it can be shown that an 18-tone scale produces much better approximations for these intervals. Accepting the possibilities of extensions in sounds and scales, how do we determine the new rules of synchronism and succession?

It is at this point, where the complexity of the problem appears to get out of hand, that computers come to our assistance, not merely as ancillary tools but as essential components in the complex process of generating auditory signals that fulfill a variety of new principles of a generalized aesthetics and are not confined to conventional methods of sound generation by a given set of musical instruments or scales nor to a given set of rules of synchronism and succession based on these very instruments and scales. The search for those new principles, algorithms, and values is, of course, in itself symbolic for our times.

I
Programs and Systems

Questions of principle are sometimes regarded as too unpractical to be important, but I suggest that this is certainly not the case in our subject.

W. ROSS ASHBY: *Principles of the Self-Organizing System*, 1962.

On-line Generation of Sound

M. DAVID FREEDMAN

Bendix Research Laboratories
Southfield, Michigan

Other articles in this book are concerned with methods of analyzing, composing, and synthesizing music on a digital computer. This article considers the specifications that a computer must meet in order to serve as an analyst of musical tones, as a composer, and as a musical instrument.

Analysis and synthesis require that the analog signals representing the sound-pressure waveform be converted into, and generated from, digital representations. This requirement places rather stringent timing demands on the input and output channels of the computer. If these operations can be accomplished in real time, the problem remains whether the computer can also carry out sufficient algorithmic processing on a time-shared basis to implement the analysis, composition, and synthesis programs. Moreover, if implemented concurrently, the algorithmic processing must not disturb the input-output processing of the analog waveforms. These are the problems facing those who must select, program, and maintain the digital computer which is to be used as an integral part of an electronic music studio installation.

ON-LINE SYNTHESIS OF TONES

On-line, real-time operation for the synthesis of computer music is highly desirable, for it gives the composer greater freedom to modify his composition while the desired results are still relatively fresh in his mind. It is especially desirable if the composer's input to the computer is made in the form of a real-time input such as a keyboard or music typewriter. However, a graphic input device is described by Mathews and Rosler elsewhere in this book.

13

To implement an on-line synthesis system the computer equipment must meet several requirements:

1. It must be accessible to the composer when he needs it.
2. The music generating equipment, such as the digital-analog converters, must be compatible with the high data rates necessary to the production of pleasant-sounding music.
3. The music being synthesized must be produced continuously in time. This requires adequate block transfer rates from auxiliary storage, a sufficiently large main storage, and, in the case of a time-shared system, a sufficiently high priority within the operating system to ensure adequate data rates.

I shall now discuss the three points listed above in greater detail.

The simplest way to ensure accessibility is to have a free-standing computer for use only as a "music console." Ideally its only users would be composers and no setup or disconnect time would be necessary. This solution, although simple, is not usually economically feasible and other solutions must be sought.

The sharing of equipment by scheduling is another approach that ensures full use of the equipment during specified hours, often during the "wee hours of the morning" when no one else cares to be bothered. This is not a permanent solution to the problem, for scheduling is becoming more difficult, and, with the new time-shared systems, complete control of the computer is usually not possible.

The final solution to all this is to have a small computer to handle the input-output functions and a large time-shared system to handle the storage and computing functions. (The problems that arise in this environment are discussed below.)

Regardless of which of these schemes is used, the music-generating equipment must be of high quality to produce pleasant sounds. This can be assured if digital-analog converters capable of converting 12 to 14 bit words at a rate of 40,000/sec are used. The long word length ensures adequate dynamic range and the high rate, a sufficiently broad frequency response. For experimenting both time and money may be saved by using a lower conversion rate, for example, 15,000 bits/sec. Although this introduces significant distortion into the audio waveforms, it does give a good indication of what the finished composition will sound like and therefore is a worthwhile approach. The final version would, of course, be produced using the higher data rate.

In order to achieve continuous reproduction without breaks in the sound, adequate block transfer rates must be provided between auxiliary storage and main memory. Here the usual procedure is to refill one block of main memory from a disk, for example, and a second block to feed data to the digital-analog converter. Thus the block transfer from the disk to the first block must be completed before the last word in the second block is sent to the converter. Since most auxiliary storage devices have fixed gaps between transfers, it may be necessary to increase the block size to overcome the effects of the gaps; thus a large main memory would be required. In a time-shared system, in which a peripheral computer is used for conversion and buffering, high priority within the large system is required to ensure that the data flow to the converter will be maintained.

We have assumed until now that a single digital-analog converter is used to convert the digital data to sound. In fact, for stereo reproduction two converters double the requirements and make all timing problems more stringent. If another type of converter is used, such as a bank of voltage-controlled oscillators, the data requirements will depend on the number of these oscillators, their configuration, and so on. In general, however, the same difficulties and problems still exist, although analysis of the system may be more complicated.

ANALYSIS OF MUSICAL TONES

The same basic digital-computer system employed for the synthesis of music can also be adapted to analysis. An analog-digital converter is necessary to translate the sound-pressure waveforms into sequences of 12 to 14 bit numbers suitable for digital processing. As in the synthesis system, the data must be transferred to storage rapidly enough to ensure that no conversion samples will be missed.

Also, as before, the conversion rate should be 40,000/sec so that no aliasing can take place. Aliasing results when partials whose frequencies exceed one-half the conversion rate are present. These partials are then folded over in the spectrum so that their apparent frequency is given by

$$f_{app} = f_c - f_{act}$$

where f_{app} is the apparent frequency of the partial, f_{act} is the actual frequency, and f_c is the conversion rate. This equation is valid in the range given by

$$\tfrac{1}{2}f_c \le f_{act} \le f_c$$

It should be added that a similar effect takes place during synthesis and is responsible for much of the distortion heard at lower conversion rates, so objectionable when an attempt is made to generate a complex waveform, such as a variable-frequency sawtooth. In this case, in addition to the desired tone, undesirable whistles are produced during the conversion process.

CONCURRENT ALGORITHM PROCESSING

In most cases the conversion processes do not use up all the available computing power of the digital computer. Thus it may be possible to implement analysis or synthesis algorithms which can operate concurrently with the converters. It must be emphasized that the continuity of the conversion processes is so important that they must be assigned the highest possible priority, with algorithmic processing being carried out only as the remaining time allows. If the generation of data for synthesis cannot keep up with the digital-analog converters, the whole scheme will fail and concurrent processing of data may not be feasible. However, it may still be possible to carry out algorithmic processing during the conversion of previously processed compositions. This procedure is a straightforward application of time-sharing a real-time job with a job involving computation only.

INTERFACES FOR A MUSIC CONSOLE

The usual method of communicating with a computer suffers from long delays between "action" and "reaction." A deck of Hollerith cards is submitted and batch processed along with other jobs. These delays range from overnight to several days and can be quite intolerable. Thus there is a need for real-time interaction between composer and computer that will result in immediate feedback.

Several devices are available to facilitate the implementation of an interface of this nature:

1. Typewriter.
2. Music typewriter.
3. Organ keyboard.
4. Graphic input device.

A standard electric typewriter or teletypewriter can be interfaced easily to most computers and the characters interpreted. Unfortunately, the composer is forced to learn the "code" for this type of communication. The music typewriter does away with this last problem by typing directly in musical notation. To my knowledge, however, no such installation exists, probably because of the complexity of implementing this special-purpose device.

A third possibility is a musical keyboard. Although organ keyboards are widely used to control analog circuits and voltage-controlled oscillators, no digital installation has been attempted, even though it need not be an overly complicated task.

A graphic-input device developed at Bell Telephone Laboratories uses a light pen to write on a cathode-ray tube. This provides a simple method of simultaneously communicating both frequency and timing information to the computer in the form of a single frequency versus time plot. (The details of this device are described by Rosler and Mathews in another article in this book.)

Output interfaces can also be quite useful; for example, the utility of a device that would automatically generate a score during composition or conversion of the music is obvious. In fact, it is possible to generate a digital tape that could be used as the input to a musical-score typesetting machine and thus automatically produce the type for printing the score.

OTHER APPLICATIONS

Analog equipment for editing and storing music is inherently of poor quality; for example, analog tapes deteriorate with time and cannot be cued accurately for purposes of montaging. On the other hand, digital tapes can be rewritten periodically, thus preventing any deterioration of the information contained in them. Moreover, if a conversion rate of 40,000 words/sec is used, cuing of tapes can be accomplished to within 25 μsec, which is more than adequate for music compositions. Thus a system of analog-digital and digital-analog converters can convert analog tapes for storage and editing and then back again for listening. Two restrictions must be observed. First, the allowed input range of the analog-digital converters must not be exceeded to prevent clipping, and, second, the results of the editing step must be normalized to prevent feeding nonsense data to the digital-analog converters. In either case serious distortions would result.

SUMMARY

In this article the basic requirements necessary to use a digital computer as a tool for analysis and synthesis of music have been presented. It is desirable to operate in an on-line mode so that the composer can interact with the system as if it were a musical instrument. Thus the composer-computer interface becomes the "console," and the computer can respond to the musician in the classical way. Other uses for the systems presented include automatic preparation of scores for printing, conversion of analog tapes into digital form for storage, and digital editing of tapes.

A Computer System for Time-Variant Harmonic Analysis and Synthesis of Musical Tones

JAMES W. BEAUCHAMP

University of Illinois
Urbana, Illinois

We may now be at the threshold of the discovery of mathematical descriptions for *beautiful tones,* as they are commonly termed in conventional music. Undoubtedly psychological and esthetical arguments exist to refute the possibility or desirability of general descriptions of beauty, but, at least in conventional music, there appears to be sufficient agreement about criteria for judging desirable tone qualities to guarantee the existence of some invariant descriptions of such qualities. Meanwhile in synthetic music we may also have criteria for beautiful sound events, but we often lack the information necessary to specify the sounds we imagine. This is especially ironic in view of the fact that with our present electronic equipment we can generate virtually any sound, given its specification.

During the last few years substantial progress has been made in developing techniques for analyzing acoustical signals. That we can record sounds with nearly impeccable fidelity and analyze them in terms of parameters that closely relate to the way we hear and provide complete mathematical descriptions of the sound signals has been established by the work described in this article and the recent work of others. This capability is based on our present electronics technology—especially our digital computer technology—and mathematical concepts that were developed more than two hundred years ago.

The Fourier series, a technique for expanding almost any function on a finite interval or a periodic function on the infinite interval in terms of an infinite sum of appropriately weighted, harmonically related sinusoids, was discovered by the French mathematician-physicist J. B. J. Fourier in 1807 in connection with a treatise on heat. The implications of the Fourier series expansion for acoustics led G. S. Ohm (1843) [1] and H. L. F. von Helmhotz (1863) [2] to investigate the hearing of musical sounds, which are quasi-periodic vibrations, in terms of the harmonic sinusoids of which they are composed. The analysis of the perception of harmonic tones [3] and the harmonic structure of musical sounds [4–6] has continued since the advent of the electronic age, but until recently these studies have been seriously limited by the lack of proper measuring equipment.

The value of the Fourier series for musical tone analysis, appropriately modified for time-variant signals, has been well demonstrated by recent work at the University of Illinois [7] and by that of two other research groups [8–10]. For each of these investigations the computer was the sole analytical tool used. Although it is possible to construct a real-time analyzer with specialized components, the computer is an attractive solution because of its flexibility and because the user does not need to purchase the hardware. In this article I discuss in detail a new musical tone analysis-synthesis system we have developed at the University of Illinois, the basic techniques we use, including some new innovations, and some preliminary conclusions based on the data derived.

THE ANALYSIS-SYNTHESIS SYSTEM

The analysis-synthesis system was, first of all, designed to process large numbers of musical tones. Only by the examination and study of a large amount of data can we expect to describe the sound output of a musical instrument over its complete dynamic and pitch ranges and take into account the variations due to style, context, and chance.

The block diagram in Figure 1 illustrates the configuration of the essential hardware and software components of the analysis system used for the investigation. The important subsystems accomplish analog-digital (A/D) conversion, Fourier series analysis, display photography of time-variant frequency, amplitudes, and phases, Fourier series synthesis, and digital-analog (D/A) conversion. The link between the analysis and synthesis is formed by card data that specify the time-variant fundamental frequency and harmonic amplitudes for each musical tone or, more efficiently, by a program called LINSEG that constructs straight-line approximations to these data and stores the end-point values on digital magnetic tape. [Because the tape format required for the computer used for analysis (CDC 1604) is completely

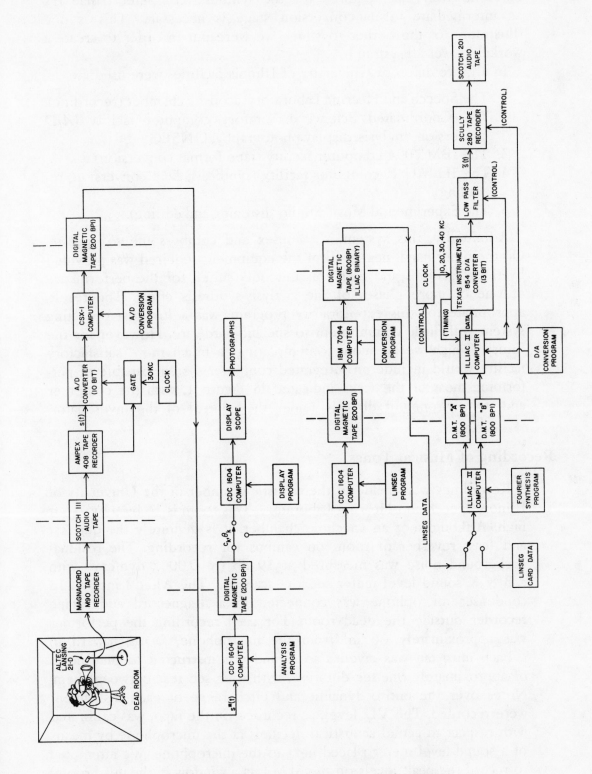

Figure 1. Computer sound analysis-synthesis system.

different from that required for the synthesis computer (Illiac II), an intermediate format-conversion stage is necessary. This is one illustration of the bother to which we were put in order to create a workable over-all system.]

In all, five different University of Illinois facilities were used:

1. The Speech and Hearing Laboratory, acoustic chamber (recording).
2. The Coordinated Science Laboratory computer facility (*A/D* conversion, analysis, display photography, LINSEG).
3. The IBM 7094 computer facility (tape format conversion).
4. The ILLIAC II computer facility (synthesis, *D/A* conversion, recording).
5. The Experimental Music Studio (listening and editing).

Admittedly, this system is complex and cumbersome to operate. On the other hand, nearly all of the equipment required was provided by these facilities and each was uniquely suited for the performance of one or more phases of the analysis-synthesis effort. The result, appropriate for this expoloratory program, was a low-cost operating system with little commitment to specific hardware. However for the future (which we are now contemplating) a much more satisfactory facility would include an integrated computer system capable of performing most of the tasks indicated in Figure 1, with the computer and its environment directly under the control of the investigator.

Recording of Musical Tones

Recordings were made in the acoustic chamber of the University of Illinois Speech and Hearing Laboratory. This room is 16 by 9 by 7½ ft high. Although not an anechoic chamber, it is definitely the quietest and least reverberant room on campus for recording. The residual background noise was measured at 19 db (re 0.0002 dyn/cm²) with a B & K sound level meter set for "scale A." The Altec Lansing 21d condenser microphone was connected to a Magnecord audio tape recorder outside the dead room. For each recording the performer was approximately 66 in. from the microphone, facing toward it.

Each musician was given a score and was instructed to play notes of approximately one-sec duration, with four sec rest between them. Notes over the entire dynamic and pitch range of each instrument were recorded. The VU level, as recorded on the tape, was calibrated with respect to actual acoustical decibels at the microphone by means of a sound-level meter placed next to the microphone. We attempted to record the peak levels on the SLM (via a window in the dead room) and to correlate them with the peak readings on the tape recorder. This proved to be very unsatisfactory, however, because of the difference between the ballistics of the two meter needles. A much better method involves calibrating with a steady tone. In the future we will record a steady tone from a loudspeaker and calibrate simultaneously by measuring the output directly from the microphone. Because of the wide dynamic ranges of some musical instruments, it was necessary for us to record at two or more gain levels. The record gain was kept constant as much as possible, but when a change was made the level was recalibrated.

A list of the tones for each musical instrument was made, and each tone was described by various data, such as dynamic marking and pitch, and given a number. Then a tape consisting of 60 of the most representative tones was extracted from the original set, and each tone in this edited tape was sequentially assigned a new four-digit octal tone number. The first two digits refer to the instrument number, and the third and fourth digits give the tone number within each instrument tone set. From this point in the analysis-synthesis procedure tones are identified only by their octal tone numbers.

Analog-to-Digital Conversion of the Musical Tones

Before describing our analog-to-digital conversion system, I should like to make a few remarks in general about A/D facilities. At present only a few computer installations for the general user in the United States have any facility for converting audio signals into corresponding digital data and for the reverse operation of converting digital data into audio signals. There are several reasons for this state of affairs:

1. The operation of A/D equipment requires special procedures.
2. The high sample rates and high quantization accuracies required for audio work have not been achievable until recently.
3. The number of potential users of such analog-digital facilities is small compared with the total population of computer users.
4. The use of analog signals has not been a part of the research interests of the people who make computer usage policy.

The facility at the Bell Telephone Laboratories in Murray Hill, New Jersey, is a notable exception. For at least 10 years the people at Bell have been experimenting with the use of computers to process sound and television signals as part of a general program in perceptual research [11, 12]. This was made possible by their use of A/D and D/A converter systems. During the last four years the technology has improved to the point at which an *A/D-D/A* converter system with the necessary speed (20,000 to 50,000 samples/sec) and the necessary quantization accuracy (10 to 13 bits) can be purchased for $4000 to $8000. For audio work *A/D* equipment is now connected to computers at M. I. T., Brooklyn Polytechnic Institute, the University of Illinois, Stanford, and U. C. L. A. I should mention that more and more computing centers are becoming interested in analog work and that for some time *A/D* (hybrid) subsystems have played important roles in specialized governmental and industrial systems—unaccessible to most researchers.

For our particular application we needed a low-cost method for converting and automatically separating a large number of musical tones. The tones were to be identified by their tone numbers and stored on digital tape.

When the University of Illinois Coordinated Science Laboratory decided in 1965 to build a 10-bit, 50-kc *A/D* converter for connection to their special computer, the CSX-1, we had the facility for such a method. In this experimental period accessibility and low-cost were of paramount importance. The computer time for the CSX-1 was free to our project, and we were able to operate the computer for as long as six consecutive hours in order to develop the necessary programs.

The CSX-1 computer is a special-purpose machine especially designed for real-time input-output communication and logical manipulation of data. However, the relatively poor arithmetic capability of the CSX-1 has restricted its usage to special experiments. The CSX-1 has 16 levels of interrupt but no direct-memory access (DMA). Without a DMA there is no chance of transferring continuously the digitized analog samples to tape in usable length records. Moreover, the digital magnetic-tape units work at 200 BPI density and are internally clocked to write 12-bit samples at a rate of 15.4 kc (assuming an infinite record length), slower than necessary for good audio work. Therefore we used core storage for the samples. It turned out that 29,952 was a convenient number of samples to work with, and at a sample rate of 30 kc this meant that the maximum length of sound which could be digitized was 0.997 sec.

The conversion system consisted of the following components.

1. An Ampex 408 audio tape recorder.
2. Some special circuitry built by our group, including a record head monitor preamp, a high-gain gate, and a 30-kc crystal oscillator.
3. The 10-bit *A/D* converter with an external clocking capability.
4. The CSX-1 computer with its associated paper-tape reader, flexowriter, printer, CRT display, and digital magnetic tape units.

Besides these hardware items, several software items necessary to the operation included the input and output media, an audio tape with recorded signals and a digital tape for storage of the digitized versions of the signals. Also required were system programs and the paper-tape sound conversion program (TONE CONVERT). The hardware configuration is shown in Figure 2.

TONE CONVERT is designed to accomplish

1. Input of the musical tone samples via the A/D converter.
2. Immediate display of this data by output to D/A converters connected to a Tektronix X-Y oscilloscope.
3. Writing the tone samples on digital data tape in blocks of 144 records, 208 samples per record.
4. Searching for a "last tone marker" and positioning the data tape just before this marker.
5. Rewinding the data tape.
6. Writing a last tone marker on the data tape (an "end file" mark).
7. Printing the data.

Since the order of use of these operations is not necessarily fixed, the flexowriter is used with the interrupt facility to cause transfer to the various portions of the program that carry out these seven oper-

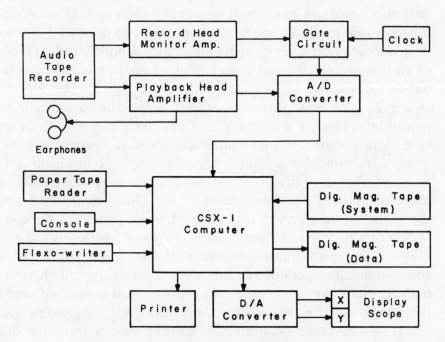

Figure 2. Sound signal A/D conversion system.

ations. All take place immediately after their respective symbols "A," "D," "W," "S," "E," and "P" are typed. However, typewriter interrupt is "locked out" during all operations except display, which occurs automatically after the end of the A/D operation.

Operation of the Conversion Program

After the system is set up, as shown in Figure 2, the program TONE CONVERT is read into the computer, and the tone number of the first of the series of tones to be converted is entered in binary at one of the console registers. When the program is initiated, it immediately goes into a "wait for interrupt" mode. The operator starts the audio tape recorder, types "A" (to cause interrupt), and monitors the sound signal through his earphones. While he hears the tone, the signal is being digitized and stored in the core memory. Immediately after the conversion the first 256 points of the converted signal appear on the display screen. By means of console switches the operator can advance or back up one frame at a time and thereby scrutinize the entire signal for accuracy of conversion. If the conversion accuracy is judged sufficient, he types "W," which causes the information to be written on digital tape.

It has been demonstrated that the beginnings or *attack* portions of musical tones are of the greatest importance to their identification [13]. It is also important to convert as much of each tone as possible. Therefore, because less than one second of signal can be stored in the CSX-1, it is necessary to start conversion immediately before the beginning of each tone as it is played back. This is accomplished by a circuit of our own design, which gates the 30 kc clock signal to the A/D converter at a fixed time after the audio signal derived from the tape recorder record head reaches a certain threshold. Since the portion of the audio tape corresponding to the beginning of the signal passes over the record head, a fraction of a second before the playback head, proper adjustment of the gate circuit threshold and time-delay control must be made to allow for proper cueing of the clock signal with respect to the audio signal derived from the playback head (to be converted).

The two conversion errors that occur most frequently are amplitude clipping and premature conversion. If the display indicates a faulty conversion, the operator readjusts the time-delay and threshold controls, rewinds the audio tape past the tone just converted, and repeats the conversion-display process. The process of digitizing each tone signal on the tape, examining its display, and writing the digital information on tape is repeated until either the digital tape is full or the audio-tone sequence is exhausted. Each tone written is identified by its tone number in the tape format, and the tone numbers are automatically augmented by 1 each time a tone is written. Note that in this system the tones are automatically segmented from one another and are easy to identify in the rest of the computer process. The entire conversion operation is summarized by the flow diagram in Figure 3. Each digital tape holds approximately 58 tones or 58 sec of information. In another adjustment the A/D converter input attenuator is set so that the peak value of the converted signal lies between the maximum and one-half the maximum possible converted value. The input attenuator is set for the voltage ranges ± 0.75, ± 1.5, ± 3.0, and ± 6.0 V. The tape recorder output gain is never changed.

In March 1967 the CSX-1 computer was transferred from the Coordinated Science Laboratory to the Physics Department of the University of Illinois. Since the A/D converter and other I/O units are no longer attached, it ceases to be available as an A/D conversion system. In the near future we expect that this system will be replaced by a computer system provided by the University of Illinois Department of Computer Science. Three provisions of the new facility will improve the efficiency and eliminate most of the manual operations necessary in the CSX-1 system:

1. Direct real-time conversion of signals onto digital tape at high density will allow up to four minutes of continuous conversion and eliminate the necessity for a gate circuit. Segmentation of tones will be accomplished by the computer.
2. Both the A/D and the D/A converters of the new system will have quantization accuracies of 13 bits and will be capable of conversion rates greater than 40 kc. Recordings to be processed by A/D conversion can be played back with the gain set such that a sine wave recorded at 0 db will utilize only the first 10 bits plus sign. As a result there will be two bits left — a safety factor of 12 db — to handle signal peaks that exceed 0 db on the recording.
3. The tape recorder will be a two-channel device, and a clock signal recorded during the actual recording of the sound signal can be used to time the A/D conversion.

Harmonic Spectrum Analysis

The digital magnetic tapes that are derived from the CSX-1 conversion system and contain the digitized musical tones serve as input media for a harmonic-analysis system programmed for the Coordinated

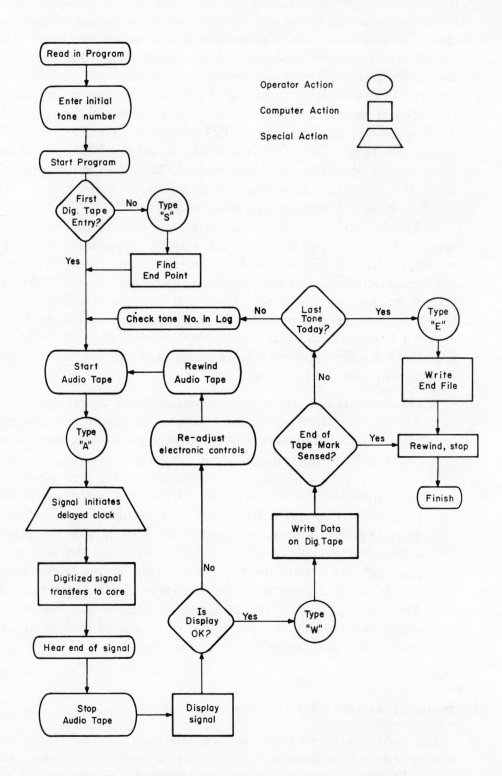

Figure 3.   Normal operating procedure for use of the A/D conversion system.

Science Laboratory's CDC 1604 computer. The object of the program ANMAG is to analyze the raw data contained on the tapes in terms of a time-variant spectral characterization and to output the results onto another set of tapes which, in turn, is processed in later steps by LINSEG and the display and postanalysis routines.

If the harmonic or Fourier series method of analysis is to be applied, it must be assumed that each of the original musical tones* can be represented by the function

$$s(t) = \sum_{k=1}^{n_h} \overline{c}_k(t) \cos \left[k2\pi \int_0^t \overline{f}_1(t)\, dt + \overline{\phi}_k(t) \right]. \tag{1}$$

Note that the harmonic amplitudes $(\overline{c}_k)$, the fundamental frequency $(\overline{f}_1)$, and the relative phases $(\overline{\phi}_k)$ are treated as time-variant parameters. In contrast, inharmonic partials and additive noise are not represented as such by this formula; if they occur in an original tone, they are manifested in the analysis as perturbations of the regular analysis parameters.

Given the sample values of $s(t)$, $s(n\,\Delta T)$, we can proceed with the analysis with the following procedure:

1. *Frequency correction.* Starting with an estimated frequency (f_e), an average frequency (f_a) is obtained by using one or more analysis passes as described.

2. *Heterodyne operation.* For each harmonic k two signals are created.

$$p_k(n\,\Delta T) = \cos(k2\pi f_a n\,\Delta T)\, s(n\,\Delta T), \tag{2a}$$

$$q_k(n\,\Delta T) = \sin(k2\pi f_a n\,\Delta T)\, s(n\,\Delta T), \quad k = 1, \ldots, n_h. \tag{2b}$$

ΔT is the sample period. $\Delta T = 1/f_s$, where f_s is the sample frequency.

3. *Filter operation.* Usually the Fourier coefficients a_k and b_k are obtained by the simple average of p_k and q_k over a single period.

$$a_k(n\,\Delta T) = \frac{2\,\Delta T}{T} \sum_{i=n-[N/2]}^{n+[(N-1)/2]} p_k(i\,\Delta T) = \frac{2}{T} \int_{n\Delta T - T/2}^{n\Delta T + T/2} p_k(t)\, dt. \tag{3a}$$

$$b_k(n\,\Delta T) = \frac{2\,\Delta T}{T} \sum_{i=n-[N/2]}^{n+[N-(1/2)]} q_k(i\,\Delta T) = \frac{2}{T} \int_{n\Delta T - T/2}^{n\Delta T + T/2} q_k(t)\, dt. \tag{3b}$$

The discrete averaging accomplished by the computer approximates

*The sounds studied in this investigation are assumed to be harmonic to a considerable degree. This includes the human voice and wind and string musical instruments but excludes nearly all percussion instruments.

the continuous case: T is the fundamental averaging period, $T = 1/f_a$, and

$$N = (T/\Delta T + 1/2)$$

is the nearest integral number of samples per period. A simulated low-pass filter, described later in this section, is sometimes used to smooth the a_k and b_k data.

4. *Right triangle solution.* The harmonic amplitudes and absolute phases are computed by the relations

$$c_k(t) = \sqrt{a_k{}^2(t) + b_k{}^2(t)}, \tag{4a}$$

$$\theta_k(t) = \begin{cases} -a \tan\left[b_k(t)/a_k(t)\right] - \pi u\left[-a_k(t)\right], a_k \neq 0, \\ -\dfrac{\pi}{2}\,\mathrm{sgn}\left[b_k(t)\right], a_k = 0, \end{cases} \tag{4b}$$

where t takes on the discrete values $n\,\Delta T$. The relative phases and the fundamental frequency are given by

$$\phi_k(t) = \theta_k(t) - k\left[\theta_1(t) - \theta_1(0)\right], \tag{5a}$$

$$f_1(t) = f_a + \left[\theta_1(t) - \theta_1(t - DT)\right]/2\pi DT. \tag{5b}$$

Only those values of $c_k(t)$, $\theta_k(t)$, and $\Delta f_1(t) = f_1(t) - f_a$ that correspond to samples every DT seconds are stored on digital tape by the analysis program. DT is some integral divisor of the average fundamental period; that is, $DT = T/M$, where M is the number of analyses to be stored per period. Since the ϕ_k values are readily derived from the more fundamental θ_k values, they are not stored. The algorithm for the Fourier analysis appears in Figure 4.

Another parameter computed and stored by the analysis program is the instantaneous rms value of the signal. In continuous representation this is given by

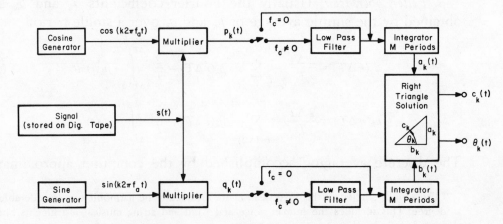

Figure 4.   Harmonic analysis algorithm.

$$s_{rms}(t) = \left(\frac{1}{T} \int_{t-T/2}^{t+T/2} s^2(t) \, dt\right)^{1/2}. \tag{6}$$

This can be compared with the frequency domain equivalent

$$\tilde{s}_{rms}(t) = \left(\frac{1}{2} \sum_{k=1}^{n_h} c_k^2(t)\right)^{1/2}, \tag{7}$$

which is not stored.

The analysis method can be explained either in the frequency or time domains, as Figure 5 illustrates. The top graph represents the Fourier transform spectrum $S(f)$ of a hypothetical musical tone $s(t)$. The spectrum consists of curves instead of line spectra because the harmonic amplitudes are assumed to vary with time.

If we wish to measure the envelope of the third harmonic of the tone, we heterodyne $s(t)$, with the frequency $3f_1$, indicated by the second graph. The third graph shows the spectrum which consists of the components of $S(f)$ folded about $3f_1$. The component centered about the vertical axis is the Fourier transform of the desired Fourier coefficient $a_3(t)$. Therefore, if we filter out the other components, we are left with just the spectrum of $a_3(t)$, as shown in the fourth graph.

The analysis technique can also be illustrated by an example in the time domain. The bottom graph shows the attack portion of another hypothetical musical tone. If we choose an arbitrary time t_0 and perform a Fourier series calculation on the interval $t_0 - T/2$ to $t_0 + T/2$, we obtain a set of Fourier coefficients a_k, b_k. The Fourier theorem states that the Fourier series converges to $s(t)$ everywhere on the open interval $(t_0 - T/2, t_0 + T/2)$. In particular, it converges for $t = t_0$. Hence, because t_0 is arbitrary, by application of the continuous version of (3), we obtain a continuum of values of a_k and b_k and the resulting time-varying Fourier series converges for all of $s(t)$:

$$s(t) = \sum_{k=1}^{\infty} a_k(t) \cos \frac{2\pi k t}{T} + b_k(t) \sin \frac{2\pi k t}{T} \tag{8a}$$

$$= \sum_{k=1}^{\infty} c_k(t) \cos \left[2\pi k \int_0^t f_1(t) \, dt + \phi_k(t)\right]. \tag{8b}$$

Although it does not necessarily follow that $\overline{c_k} = c_k$, $\overline{f_1} = f_1$, and $\overline{\phi_k} = \phi_k$, it is true that if these parameters are changing slowly, compared with the fundamental period, they will be nearly equal [14].

The calculation of (3) is convenient for the computer, because once a_k ($[N/2] \, \Delta T$) and b_k ($[N/2] \, \Delta T$) are computed successive values of a_k and b_k can be computed by using the recursion relation

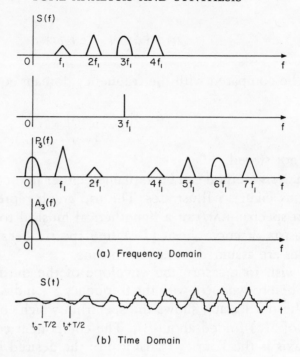

(a) Frequency Domain

(b) Time Domain

Figure 5. Graphic representation of the analysis process.

$$a_k(n\,\Delta T) = a_k[(n-1)\,\Delta T] + \frac{2\Delta T}{T}\left\{p_k\left[\left(n+\frac{N-1}{2}\right)\Delta T\right] - p_k\left[\left(n-1-\frac{N}{2}\right)\Delta T\right]\right\},$$
(9a)

$$b_k(n\,\Delta T) = b_k[(n-1)\,\Delta T] + \frac{2\Delta T}{T}\left\{q_k\left[\left(n+\frac{N-1}{2}\right)\Delta T\right] - q_k\left[\left(n-1-\frac{N}{2}\right)\Delta T\right]\right\}.$$
(9b)

The values of p_k and q_k are computed by (2) and the cosine and sine functions are computed by the recursion relations

$$\cos\left[(n+1)\,\Delta T\right] = \cos(\Delta T)\cos(n\,\Delta T) - \sin(\Delta T)\sin(n\,\Delta T), \qquad (10a)$$

$$\sin\left[(n+1)\,\Delta T\right] = \sin(\Delta T)\cos(n\,\Delta T) + \cos(\Delta T)\sin(n\,\Delta T). \qquad (10b)$$

However, it is not feasible to store information corresponding to the same number of samples per second as the original conversion sample frequency. For one thing, this would result in many times more data at the output of the analysis system as there was at the input. Generally, at the most only a few samples per period T are stored. Therefore in actual practice (9) is replaced by a procedure for adding and subtracting "blocks" of information for each analysis sample computed. If we assume for simplicity that $T = N \cdot \Delta T$, $N = KM$, and M samples per period are to be generated, the jth block for $a_k(t)$ is calculated by

$$\text{BLOCK } (j) = \sum_{i=jK+1}^{(j+1)K} p_k(i\,\Delta T). \qquad (11)$$

Equation (9a) is then replaced by

$$a_k(j \cdot DT) = a_k((j-1) \cdot DT) + \frac{2}{N}\left[\text{BLOCK}\left(j + \frac{M}{2}\right) - \text{BLOCK}\left(j - \frac{M}{2}\right)\right], \qquad (12)$$

where $DT = K \cdot \Delta T$ is the time between samples.

If T is not an even integral multiple of ΔT, modification of (11) is required; this is accomplished by the program ANMAG.

The filter frequency response corresponding to the averaging operation given by (3) is

$$H(j\omega) = \frac{\sin (\omega T/2)}{(\omega T/2)}, \qquad \omega = 2\pi f. \qquad (13)$$

We see, in reference to Figure 5 (in which $f_1 = 1/T$), that although this transfer function is zero for all integral multiples of f_1 and will provide a perfect filter for periodic signals whose spectral components are pure lines the transfer function will not filter out the entire spectral envelopes of the components that correspond to a time-variant signal. The result of this imperfection is that the analyzed parameters will contain ripple with an apparent frequency f_1 superimposed on the parameter contours of interest (14). This effect can be alleviated considerably by a filter with monotonically decreasing frequency response, such as the well-known third-order Butterworth low-pass filter. The amplitude frequency response of this filter is given by

$$|H(j2\pi f) = \frac{1}{\sqrt{1 + (f/f_c)^6}}, \qquad (14)$$

where f_c is the cutoff frequency. Using Z transform technique (15), we can derive a recursion formula that will simulate this filter for discrete data:

$$a_k(n \; \Delta T) = x_1 p_k[(n-1) \; \Delta T] + x_2 p_k[(n-2) \; \Delta T] - y_1 a_k[(n-1) \; \Delta T]$$
$$- y_2 a_k[(n-2) \; \Delta T] - y_3 a_k[(n-3) \; \Delta T], \qquad (15a)$$

where

$$x_1 = \omega_c \; \Delta T \; e^{-\omega_c \Delta T/2}\left[-\cos\left(\sqrt{3\omega_c}\frac{\Delta T}{2}\right) + \frac{1}{\sqrt{3}}\sin\left(\sqrt{3\omega_c}\frac{\Delta T}{2}\right)\right] + e^{-\omega_c \Delta T},$$

$$x_2 = \omega_c \; \Delta T \; e^{-3\omega_c \Delta T/2}\left[\cos\left(\sqrt{3\omega_c}\frac{\Delta T}{2}\right) + \frac{1}{\sqrt{3}}\sin\left(\sqrt{3\omega_c}\frac{\Delta T}{2}\right)\right] + e^{-\omega_c \Delta T}, \qquad (15b)$$

$$y_1 = -\left[e^{-\omega_c \Delta T} + 2e^{-\omega_c \Delta T/2}\cos\left(\sqrt{3\omega_c}\frac{\Delta T}{2}\right)\right],$$

$$y_2 = 2e^{-3\omega_c \Delta T/2}\cos\left(\sqrt{3\omega_c}\frac{\Delta T}{2}\right) + e^{-\omega_c \Delta T},$$

$$y_3 = -e^{-2\omega_c \Delta T} \quad \text{and} \quad \omega_c = 2\pi f_c.$$

When signals are time-variant in frequency and amplitude, considerably smoother parameter curves can be made if the Butterworth low-pass filter is used in addition to taking the simple average over a period. On the other hand, we pay well for the use of this filter in terms of computation time, since each recursion requires five multiplications and four additions.

The analysis frequency f_a is determined by one or more repetitions of the analysis process. Beginning at $t = T_s$ sec ($t = 0$ corresponds to the initial signal sample) the signal is analyzed by using an estimated frequency f_e as the initial value of f_a. In this case only the absolute phase for harmonic 1 is computed and only for a number of signal samples corresponding to T_{fc} sec. Usually T_s and T_{fc} are specified in the program, but a program section that will determine these parameters by examination of the signal levels in a preliminary pass is available.

Because the instantaneous frequency $f_1(t)$ is equal to the derivative of the total phase, that is,

$$f_1(t) = \frac{d}{dt}\left[f_a t + \frac{1}{2\pi}\theta_1(t)\right] = f_a + \frac{1}{2\pi}\frac{d}{dt}\theta_1(t), \tag{16}$$

it is clear that the best average frequency for analysis would be the average of $f_1(t)$ as given by (16). Therefore the corrected average frequency is the previously assumed average frequency plus the average slope of $\theta_1(t)$ over 2π:

$$f_a \leftarrow f_a + \text{ave}\left[\frac{1}{2\pi}\frac{d}{dt}\theta_1(t)\right]. \tag{17}$$

We must be careful about the singularities produced when $\theta_1(t)$ jumps between zero and 2π. If we average the slope over T_{fc} sec, we must in essence reconstruct $\theta_1(t)$ by adding or subtracting multiples of 2π to it in order to remove these discrete jumps. However, this is equivalent to the following process:

$$\text{av}\left[\frac{1}{2\pi}\frac{d}{dt}\theta_1(t)\right] = \frac{1}{2\pi T_{fc}}\int_{T_s}^{T_s+T_{fc}}\frac{d}{dt}\theta_1(t)\,dt \tag{18}$$

$$= \frac{1}{2\pi n T_{fc}}\left[\theta_1(T_s + T_{fc}) - \theta_1(T_s) + 2\pi N_j\right],$$

where N_j is the net number of jumps of $\theta_1(t)$ between zero and 2π over the time interval.

Equation 17 gives a corrected average frequency which can in turn be used as the assumed frequency for another frequency correction. This process is repeated until two successive corrected frequencies differ by no more than 0.3%. Since f_e, the initial value of f_a, is assumed to be equal to the standard frequency supposedly intended by the performer of the musical tone under analysis, convergence generally takes place within two or three iterations. Since $\theta_1(t)$ is derived from the arc tangent of the quotient of $a_1(t)$ and $b_1(t)$, we might be led to think that convergence would not be good for cases in which the first harmonic is weak. However, we have found that convergence is good even when $c_1(t)$ is substantially below the level of the other harmonics. On the other hand, Δf_1, which is computed from θ_1, does exhibit a large amount of noise when c_1 is small.

In summary, the ANMAG program operates on the signal samples stored on the digital magnetic tape supplied by the CSX-1 conversion system. Additional input data on paper tape consists of the following:

1. f_e, the estimated fundamental frequency.
2. n_h, the number of harmonics to be analyzed (based on known formant properties of the instruments).
3. M, the number of analyses to be stored per period.
4. AD, the A/D full-scale voltage during conversion.

Each set of values corresponds to a particular tone number. The program prints out the following set of auxiliary data:

1. NTONE, the tone number.
2. f_s.
3. f_e.
4. T_s and T_{fc}.
5. A record of the frequency corrections.
6. The final corrected frequency f_a.
7. Deviation of f_a from the nearest standard frequency measured in cents.
8. CORCON $= AD/6$.
9. $DT = T/M$.
10. The maximum values of $s_{rms}, \bar{s}_{rms}, c_1, \ldots, c_{n_h}$ and the times at which the maxima occur.

The analysis data for each tone are written by ANMAG in the following order: n_h, NTONE; f_a; DT; CORCON; $s_{rms}(0)$, $\Delta f_1(0)$, $c_1(0)$, $\theta_1(0)$, $c_2(0)$, $\theta_2(0)$, $\ldots$, $c_{n_h}(0)$, $\theta_{n_h}(0)$; $\ldots$; $s_{rms}(T_L)$, $\Delta f_1(T_L)$, $c_1(T_L)$, $s_1(T_L)$, $\ldots$, $c_{n_h}(T_L)$, $\theta_{n_h}(T_L)$. ($T_L = DT \cdot [29{,}952 \cdot \Delta T/DT]$.) The over-all logic of the analysis program is given in Figure 6.

The Display System

The tremendous task of correlating all of the data generated by an

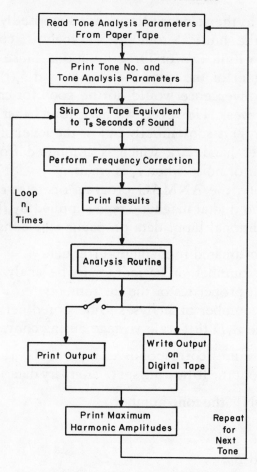

Figure 6.   Overall logic of analysis program (ANMAG).

analysis of musical tones makes it necessary to find an efficient method of plotting the frequency, amplitude, and phase graphs. Printer graphs are too slow and clumsy to work with and CAL-COMP, in spite of its attractive features, is too slow for recording 2000 graphs per musical instrument. Consequently we were very pleased when the Coordinated Science Laboratory decided to build a special-purpose display apparatus for connection to their CDC 1604 computer. The front panel of this apparatus consists of a large display screen for visual monitoring and a small, high-resolution screen for photography. It includes wired-in circuits for automatic character generation as specified by BCD code and for automatic plotting of straight lines between specified points. The information displayed is cycled continuously from an X and a Y buffer by means of a direct-memory-access arrangement.

While the display is in use, the computer can be controlled by a console typewriter located next to it, and by placing a Honeywell Pentax 35mm camera (capable of 36 consecutive frames) on a scope-camera mount of our own design we can employ the computer display system to take about 500 pictures per hour. Each graph plotted is obtained from the digital magnetic tape generated by the ANMAG program (see Figure 1).

The display program, called SEQDISP because of its automatic sequential display feature, is operated according to the following procedure:

1. After the program is loaded control is transferred to the display console typewriter.

2. The operator, in response to a typewriter request, specifies, via the typewriter, which of five parameter types is to be displayed. The five parameter types are (a) linear amplitude [labeled RMSIN for $s_{rms}(t)$ and HAR NO. K AMP for $c_k(t)$], (b) amplitude in decibels [labeled DBIN and DB HAR NO. K for $20 \log_{10}(s_{rms}/512)$ and $20 \log_{10}(c_k/512)$, respectively], (c) Δf_1 (labeled DF1), (d) $\theta_k(t)$ (labeled HAR NO. K TH), (e) $\phi_k(t)$ (labeled HAR NO. K PH).

3. In response to a typewriter request the operator types a four-digit octal tone number which specifies the first tone to be displayed.

4. A sequence of graphs is produced and photographed by periodic alternation of five manual operations: (a) press the typewriter carriage return; (this causes the next graph to be traced continuously over the display screen); (b) open camera shutter; (c) press the typewriter space bar (this causes four traces of the graph to be executed across the camera scope screen, and the film is exposed); (d) close camera shutter; (e) advance one frame. If all parameter types are requested, the graphs are displayed in the order s_{rms}, $db[s_{rms}]$, Δf_1, c_1, $db[c_1]$, θ_1, c_2, $db [c_2]$, θ_2, $\phi_2, \ldots, c_{n_h}$, $db [c_{n_h}]$, θ_{n_h}, ϕ_{n_h}. When the carriage return is depressed after the display of ϕ_{n_h}, the data for the next tone is read from the magnetic tape and the first requested parameter for this tone is displayed. In this way all data on the tape generated by ANMAG can be displayed and photographed without noticeable interruption.

5. It is also possible by means of typewriter control for the operator to change at any time the list of parameter types to be displayed, to skip forward to a new tone number, or to skip to the display of a specified harmonic number within the current tone displayed. In each case sequential displaying of the parameters can be resumed by use of the carriage return.

All of the control by typewriter is facilitated by means of the interrupt capability of the CDC 1604. Thus, whenever a special directive is typed, together with some numerical information, the information is read in and control is immediately transferred to the subroutine specified by the directive symbol. This method of computer control,

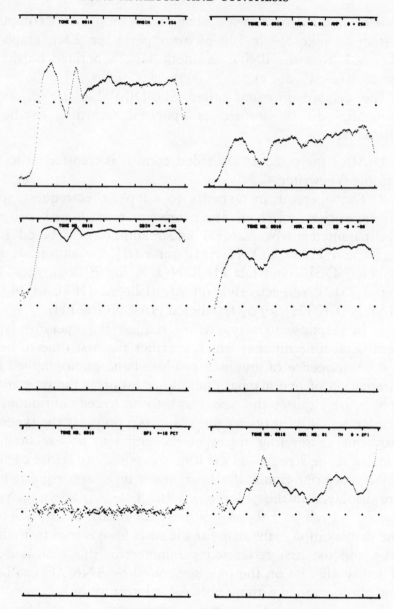

Figure 7.   Example of display output for a flute tone, $f_a = 400$ cps. (Twelve individual pictures are combined).

which also played a major role in the CSX-1 conversion program, is most desirable for effective man-machine communication.

An example of the photographs obtained from the display system is shown in Figure 7. The film-processing system was designed to provide us with 3½ by 5 in. black-on-white background prints for a total film-development-printing cost of 8.3 cents each. Normally six prints are joined together to form each 8½ x 11 page from which high-contrast Xerox copies can be made. Note that each graph is

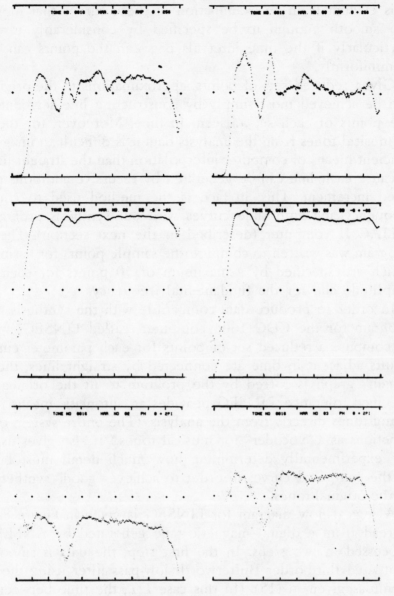

Figure 7. *(continued).*

defined by its tone number, its harmonic number (except RMSIN, DBIN, and DF1), the parameter name, and vertical scale range (upper right corner). The horizontal scale range is always 0 to 1 sec.

Linseg, A Program for Approximating Parameter Graphs in Terms of Connected Line Segments

Each parameter graph computed by the previously described Fourier series analysis system consists of between 600 and 2000 points. However it is evident from an examination of these curves that most of them are smooth enough to be specified by considerably fewer points, particularly if the time intervals between the points can be chosen nonuniformly.

Given reduced sets of points, approximations to the original graphs can be achieved most simply by constructing line segments between the points of each set adjacent in time. Moreover, for the synthesis of musical tones from the analysis data it is difficult to imagine a more efficient means of computer interpolation than the straight-line method because each line can be generated by recursive additions of a single fixed increment. This, in fact, is the method used to compute the frequency and amplitude curves with our synthesis program for the ILLIAC II computer (described in the next section). The synthesis program was written to compute the sample points for harmonic tones which are specified by a maximum of 50 points for each harmonic amplitude and for the fundamental frequency.

In order to produce data compatible with the synthesis program, a program for the CDC 1604 computer, called LINSEG, was written to compute a reduced set of points for each parameter curve. When points adjacent in time are connected by straight lines, the resulting "chain" graph is forced by the program to fit the original within a specified tolerance. LINSEG provides an automatic means for synthesizing tones directly from the analysis. (The entire system of Figure 1 functions as a "vocoder" for musical tones.) It also gives us a method for experimentally determining how much detail must be retained in the computed curves in order to achieve "good" synthetic replicas of the original tones.

A logical flow diagram for LINSEG is given in Figure 8. The data is read from a digital magnetic tape generated by ANMAG and is processed in two steps. In the first step, the data is smoothed by a simulated third-order Butterworth low-pass filter using the recursion formulas given in (15). (In this case DT, the time between adjacent parameter points, replaces ΔT, the sample period, and f_c is typically between 20 and 50 msec.) In the second step the smoothed parameter graphs are fitted by chain graphs, each consisting of a series of connected straight-line segments. Because of the necessity for handling the many special cases that can occur in the data, the algorithm devised for this second computation is quite complex.

Four constants specified by typewriter input are used to determine the accuracy of fit to the smoothed graphs: THRESH, NPIN, TOLA, and TOLF. The lowest and highest times (time is measured by the index J) for which a graph exceeds THRESH defines the time interval over which the chain graph approximation is valid.

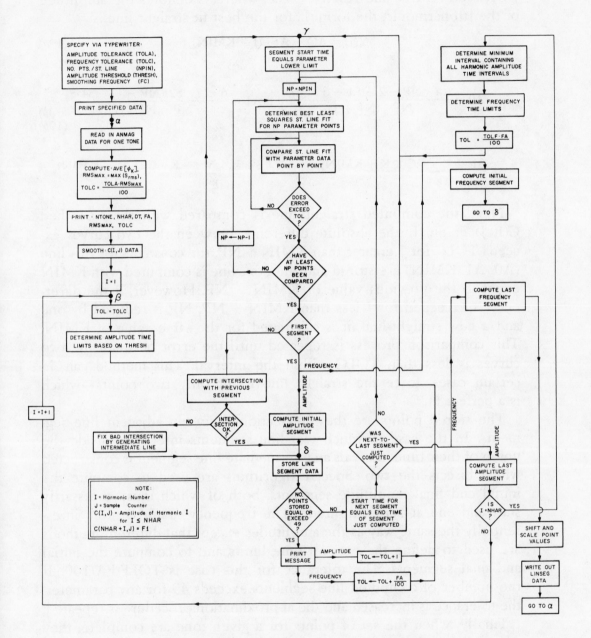

Figure 8. Logical flow diagram for LINSEG.

41

Initially, each straight line is constructed as the best least-squares fit to NP = NPIN data points. In general, given values of C(I, J) for J between KMIN and KMIN + NP, where C denotes the amplitude of the Ith harmonic, the formula for the best fit straight line is

$$Y(J) = AO + A1 \cdot (J - KMIN), \qquad (19a)$$

where

$$A0 = \frac{((4 \cdot NP - 2) \cdot S1 - 6 \cdot S2),}{NP \cdot (NP + 1)} \qquad A1 = \frac{6 \cdot (2 \cdot S2/(NP - 1) - S1),}{NP \cdot (NP + 1)}$$

$$(19b)$$

$$S1 = \sum_{K=0}^{NP-1} C(I, K + KMIN), \qquad S2 = \sum_{K=0}^{NP-1} K \cdot C(I, K + KMIN).$$

Next, the computed straight line is compared with the smoothed C(I, J) graph. If the absolute difference between the two curves exceeds TOLC for J greater than KMIN + NP, the constants for this line (A0, A1, KMIN) are stored and the next line is computed with KMIN equal to the previous value of KMIN + NP. However, if the difference is exceeded for J less than KMIN + NP, NP is reduced by one and a new straight-line fit is calculated for the same value of KMIN. This comparison process is repeated until the error between the two curves is less than TOLC within the interval. This method can, in certain cases, force the straight line to fit only two points—which is a perfect fit.

The stored points are the intersections between adjacent line segments. In the case in which two line segments intersect outside the union of their time intervals an intermediate line segment is constructed which bisects the two. Special algorithms are used to compute the initial and final amplitude segments, both of which must necessarily start and end at zero amplitude. The frequency graph is fitted in essentially the same way as the amplitudes except that different methods are used to define the over-all time limits and to compute the initial and final segments. The tolerance for this ease is TOLF·FA/100. If the number of computed line segments exceeds 49 for any parameter, the tolerance is increased and the approximation procedure is repeated.

Finally, when the set of points for a given tone are complete, they are scaled and then printed out and written onto digital magnetic tape in a BCD format identical to that of the card images used as data input for the Illiac II harmonic synthesis program. Figure 9 shows the result of LINSEG approximation in two stages, the smoothed version of an original harmonic amplitude curve and the chain graph approximation to it. The constants for this case were TOLC = 1.3, THRESH = 4, NPIN = 10, and FC = 20.

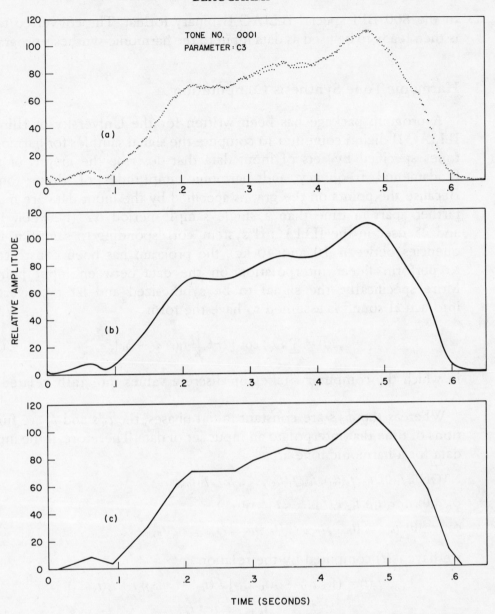

Figure 9.   Three forms of parameter data: (*a*) original data curve; (*b*) original curve smoothed by filter operation; (*c*) smoothed curve fit by series of straight-line segments.

Tape Conversion Program

Because the ILLIAC II computer was not designed to read BCD information or any of the usual binary modes and the system monitor for the ILLIAC II does not allow the computer to read tapes recorded at 200 BPI (the density used with the CDC 1604 and CSX-1 computers), we were forced to write a program for the IBM 7094 to convert the tapes generated by LINSEG from the 200 BPI BCD format to the 800 BPI special ILLIAC II binary format. The converted tape is then ready to be used as data input to the harmonic-synthesis program.

Harmonic Tone Synthesis Computation

A program package has been written for the University of Illinois ILLIAC II digital computer to compute the signal samples for harmonic tones specified by sets of input data that describe the graphs of the fundamental frequency and harmonic amplitudes of these tones. Because the points on the graphs specified by the input data are much farther apart in time than a single sample period ΔT (between 100 and 25 μsec in the ILLIAC II system, corresponding to sampling frequencies between 10 and 40 kc), the program has been constructed to perform linear interpolation on the data between input points. More specifically, the signal to be synthesized and later converted into actual sound is assumed to have the form

$$\tilde{s}(t) = \sum_{k=1}^{n_h} c_k(t) \cos \left[2\pi k \int_0^t f_1(t)\, dt + \phi_k \right], \qquad (20)$$

in which the computer t takes on discrete values integrally related to ΔT.

Whereas the ϕ_k's are constant initial phases, the c_k's and f_1 are functions of time that interpolate an input set of data. Therefore, if the input data for a harmonic tone are

NTONE, $f_1(0)$, t_{01}, $f_1(t_{01})$, t_{02}, $f_1(t_{02})$, . . ., t_{0m_0}, $f_1(t_{0m_0})$,

ϕ_1, $c_1(0)$, t_{11}, $c_1(t_{11})$, t_{12}, $c_1(t_{12})$, . . . , t_{1m_1}, $c_1(t_{1m_1})$,

ϕ_{n_h}, $c_{n_h}(0)$, $t_{n_h 1}$, $c_{n_h}(t_{n_h 1})$, $t_{n_h 2}$, $c_{n_h}(t_{n_h 2})$, . . ., $t_{n_h m_{n_h}}$, $c_{n_h}(t_{n_h m_{n_h}})$, $\qquad (21)$

we have $c_k(t)$ computed by the relation

$$c_k(t) = \left([c_k(t_{kj}) - c_k(t_{k\,j-1})] \Big/ (t_{kj} - t_{k\,j-1}) \right) t + c_k(t_{k\,j-1}),$$
$$t_{k\,j-1} \le t \le t_{kj}, \qquad (22)$$

and $f_1(t)$ is computed by an analogous formula.

The input data can be supplied by IBM data cards or by a digital tape created indirectly by LINSEG (see the preceding section). Besides the data given in List 21, the user must specify the sampling frequency and — in the case of digital tape input — the first and last tone numbers to be processed. A large number of tones can be synthesized in this manner. Each set of tone data begins with its identifying tone number, and each of the data sets is separated by a card which indicates that the tone specification has ended and gives the duration of silence (rest) generated between the preceding and succeeding tones.

The tone synthesis program package consists of a closed main program, which we hereafter refer to as the PREDIGESTER, and several open subroutines used to compute and store samples of $s(t)$. Basically, the computation is split up into two steps, which are accomplished by the PREDIGESTER and by FORSYN, the main computation subroutine. The PREDIGESTER is written in FORTRAN; it serves to call the other subroutines and to perform the first pass of computations on the input data. The output data produced by the PREDIGESTER program consist of initial values for each of the harmonic amplitudes and phases and incremental changes in these values. This second type of data is transmitted periodically to FORSYN at intervals corresponding to 1 msec. FORSYN operates on this data in the following manner:

Let FS be the number of output signal samples that occur in 1 msec (the sampling frequency divided by 1000). Further, let Δc_k and $\Delta\theta_k$ be the incremental changes for each harmonic k that are valid during this 1 msec interval and assume that a cosine table has been previously loaded so that

$$\cos_q = \cos\frac{q2\pi}{4096}, \qquad q = 0,\ldots, 4095. \tag{23}$$

The absolute values of the phases (θ_k) should be normalized to the range $(0, 4096)$ in order to facilitate the look-up operation. Then, for each sample $\tilde{s}(n\,\Delta\mathrm{T}) = \tilde{s}_n$, FORSYN computes

$$c_k \;\leftarrow c_k + \Delta c_k, \tag{24a}$$
$$\theta_k \leftarrow \theta_k + \Delta\theta_k, \tag{24b}$$
$$q_k = [\theta_k]^*, \qquad \text{for } k = 1,\ldots, n_h, \tag{24c}$$

and

$$s_n = \sum_{k=1}^{n_h} c_k \cdot \cos_{q_k}. \tag{24d}$$

Each sample is written on digital tape via an output buffer. These operations are repeated until FS samples have been generated, whereupon FORSYN accepts from the PREDIGESTER a new set of values for Δc_k and $\Delta\theta_k$.

Meanwhile the PREDIGESTER derives values for Δc_k and $\Delta\theta_k$ from the input data given by List 21. The initial values of θ_k are computed by

$$\theta_k(0) = 4096 \cdot \frac{\phi_k}{2\pi}. \tag{25}$$

If we assume the definitions $c_{kj} = c_k(t_{kj})$, $t_{k0} = 0$, $c_{0j} = f_1(t_j)$, PRE-

---

*That is, the integer part of θ_k.

DIGESTER computes the slopes of the line segments of all the chain graphs that define the input data as follows:

$$M_{kj} = \begin{cases} \dfrac{c_{k\,j+1} - c_{kj}}{t_{k\,j+1} - t_{kj}}, & \text{for } j = 0, \ldots, m_k - 1; \\ 0, & \text{for } j = m_k; \\ & k = 0, \ldots, n_h. \end{cases} \tag{26}$$

A counter p is used to keep track of the 1-msec time intervals. Initially set to zero, p is increased by one each time a new set of Δc_k and $\Delta \theta_k$ values is computed and transmitted to FORSYN, and each time p is increased the fundamental frequency is increased by the relation

$$f_1 \leftarrow 0.001 \cdot M_{0j_0} + f_1. \tag{27}$$

The value j_k is the line segment end-point counter for the kth harmonic, except when k equals zero; j_0 is the corresponding counter for f_1. Note that with the input data both f_1 and the c_k's are assumed to change linearly within segments. However, with the FORSYN computation during the 1-msec intervals, the c_k's and the θ_k's are changing linearly, whereas f_1, which is determined by (27), stays fixed during this period. The fixed increments of c_k and θ_k are given by

$$\Delta c_k = M_{kj_j} \cdot \Delta T,$$
$$\Delta \theta_k = 4096 \cdot k \cdot f_1 \cdot \Delta T, \qquad k = 1, \ldots, n_h. \tag{28}$$

After each set of data given by (28) has been computed and transmitted to FORSYN, $0.001p$ is compared with $t_{k\,j_k\,+\,1}$ for each k to test for equality with any of the segment end points. If for any k this is true, we increase j_k by 1 and automatically select the appropriate new slope values given by M_{kj_k}. However, if any resulting j_k is equal to the corresponding terminal segment number m_k, $M_{km} = 0$ by (26) and we set $t_{km_k\,+\,1} = t_{0m_0}$; this prevents any further change in the appropriate values. In particular, if $j_0 = m_0$, the next millisecond of samples is the last to be computed for the current tone because the duration of the frequency parameter spans the duration of the harmonic amplitudes.

As the preceding paragraphs describe, PREDIGESTER and FORSYN are the two main parts of the harmonic-synthesis program. The main logic and the most complicated arithmetic calculations are contained in PREDIGESTER, which is written in FORTRAN. This has made the programming flexible and easy to modify; for instance, FORSYN could readily be rewritten for the synthesis of *inharmonic* tones, since the values of $\Delta \theta_k$ do not necessarily need to be integrally related to f_1. Although the object program generated by FORTRAN with the ILLIAC II is quite inefficient, it should be remembered that the bulk of the computation is done by FORSYN, which is written in machine language. In FORSYN only the simplest operations are required, such as addition, indexing, modulo indexing, and "test and jump on zero value." Because the indexing is accomplished in fast registers with the ILLIAC II, the FORSYN operations can be very fast indeed. Experiments made thus far have indicated that the computation-time/real-time ratio for harmonic tone synthesis experiments can be computed approximately by the relation

$$\frac{T_c}{T_r} = (n_h + 1) \cdot \frac{FS}{8}; \tag{29}$$

hence a one-second tone composed of 11 harmonics generated at 40 kc would take 60 sec to compute, more or less, depending on the number of segments used in the chain graphs.

Digital-Analog Conversion of Computed Tones

The conversion of the computed samples for the synthetic tones is accomplished by the ILLIAC II analog I/O interface system illustrated at the bottom of Figure 1. The conversion normally takes place immediately after the computation, although the two are separate operations. Until recently, we used two digital tapes to record the sample information to achieve a 40 kc sample rate. The information is written on each tape according to the standard ILLIAC II binary format, which is equivalent to 1024 samples per record. Since the write-read rate of the tape units used (IBM 729 VI) is 40,000 samples/sec, we can achieve this rate only if two tapes are read concurrently; that is, a record of samples is read from one tape while the other is pausing momentarily at a record gap and vice versa. Thus the continuous flow of samples that defines the sound output is broken up into blocks of 1024 samples, which are recorded alternately on tapes "A" and "B."

To maintain a steady flow of conversion samples synchronous with the crystal-derived clock signal, the tape blocks need to be stored temporarily (buffered) in core storage before conversion. While one tape unit is filling one block, the other block is ready to be converted by the analog interface; then, while the second block is filled by the other tape unit, the first block is converted to an analog signal. The computer is left free to control the output operations synchronous with the clock, whereas the tape reads directly into the core via a direct-memory-access channel. It is necessary for the CPU only to initiate the tape read operation. If the conversion rate is lower than 40 kc, each tape-filling operation terminates before the corresponding A/D conversion is completed. However, at 40 kc the operation becomes critical, and, for this reason four 1024 sample buffers are used. Theoretically, with this system an 80 kc conversion rate could be achieved.

It was found in practice that the digital tape conversion system, as originally programmed, was severely limited by its susceptibility to tape errors. One type of error in particular, called a "p-stop error," occurs when a piece of oxide obliterates a section of tape. The tape channel operates on this section as if it were a record gap. The result is that the alternation between records on tapes "A" and "B" is thrown out of proper sequence and the analog signal from this point on is hopelessly distorted.

For this reason a program was written recently to perform conversions by using only one digital tape [16]. In this case a p-stop error will cause only an audible "click" in the sound output and will not ruin the rest of the signal.

Testing of the Analysis-Synthesis System

To determine the accuracy of our analysis system and detect any gross errors that might have occurred, it was necessary to perform several different diagnostic tests. So far the system has passed all of these tests in good form.

Obviously one of the first tests to be performed was a determination of the accuracy of the analysis algorithm. For this purpose we generated an artificial transient harmonic tone of the following functional form:

$$s(t) = (1 - e^{-50t}) \cos (2\pi 510t) + 10 (1 - e^{-20t}) \sin (4\pi 510t), \qquad (30)$$

where t is in seconds.

In Figure 10, curve A shows the plot of the original first harmonic envelope $(1 - e^{-50t})$, curve B shows the analysis for the first harmonic amplitude by using simple integration over one period (to the nearest sample at $f_s = 30,000$ cps), and curve C shows the analysis by using a single-period integration followed by the Butterworth filter, as given by (15) with $f_c = 153$ cps.

Although the simple integral analysis yields a curve that contains a significant amount of ripple, the result of combining this analysis with the Butterworth filter is a curve that lies extremely close to the original with no perceptible ripple. This is true even though the first harmonic amplitude is much lower than the second. The ripple is due primarily to the transient nature of the signal [14] and secondarily to the fact that the fundamental frequency (510 cps) is not an integral divisor of the sample frequency. If we choose the fundamental equal to 500 cps, the ripple will decrease to zero after a period of time, whereas for 510 cps

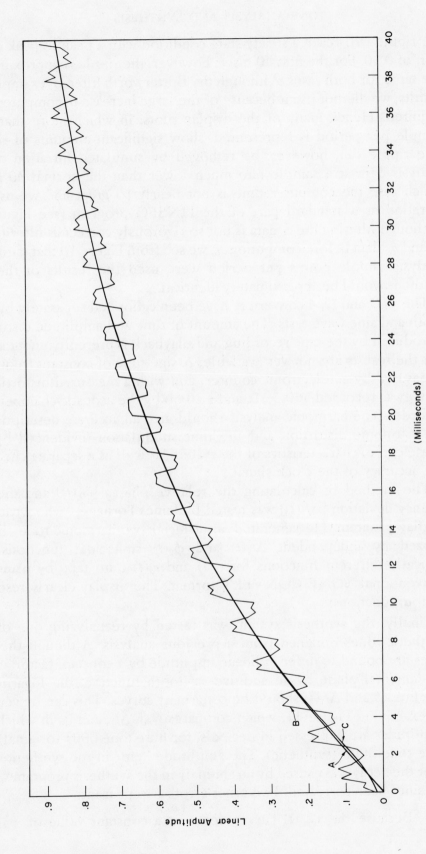

Figure 10.   Results of first harmonic analysis of the function defined in text.

the ripple will reach a steady-state condition with a peak-to-peak deviation of 0.10. For the first 40 msec, however, the ripple is approximately the same for both cases. Although the Butterworth filter gives improved results, we did not use it because of the large increase in computer time required. Hence many of the display plots, in which more than one sample per period is represented, show significant amounts of ripple. The ripple can, however, be removed by simulated filtration of the analysis data at a sample rate much lower than the normal 30 kc, in which case the computer time is not nearly so great and we use the filtration as a standard part of the LINSEG program (see Figure 9). Although filtering the c_k data is not so rigorously correct as filtering the a_k and b_k data before computing c_k, we see from Figure 10 that if enough analysis sample points per period were used the results of the two methods would be approximately identical.

The A/D and D/A converters have been calibrated separately by sawtooth and sine wave tests. The amount of time and amplitude distortion introduced by the tape recording and playback is presently under study, but the results are not yet available. A sine tone of constant frequency (measured by an electronic counter) and with a measured distortion of 0.2% was recorded at 0, −10, and −20 db by the acoustic-chamber tape recorder. The harmonic analysis should give an accurate description of the harmonic distortion and the time modulation (evidenced by the phase curve) characteristics of the system, as well as a separate check on the accuracy of the clock signal.

The method of calculating the relative phases $[\phi_k(t)]$ and the frequency deviation $[\Delta f_1(t)]$ was tested by James Fornango, who wrote the display program. He generated an artificial two-harmonic tone characterized by independent $\Delta f_1(t)$ and $\phi_2(t)$ sinusoidal functions and radically different functions for $c_1(t)$ and $c_2(t)$ onto tape by using the conventional TONE CONVERT format. The display clearly resolved all four functions.

Finally, the synthesis system was tested by reanalyzing one of the synthetic tones obtained from a previous analysis. Although the two cases are bound to differ in linear amplitude by a constant factor and in fundamental phase by an additive sawtooth function, the logarithmic amplitudes and $\Delta f_1(t)$ should be congruent curves. This can be verified by examining Figure 11, which compares s_{rms}, Δf_1, and c_3, in which the amplitudes are expressed in decibels, for flute tone 0001 (original) and flute tone 0000 (synthetic). The amplitude "pip" in the synthetic tone after the decay was caused by an anomaly in the synthesis program which has since been corrected. Two other errors are apparent:

1. Because the $s_{rms}(t)$ curves decay to a constant value of −33 db

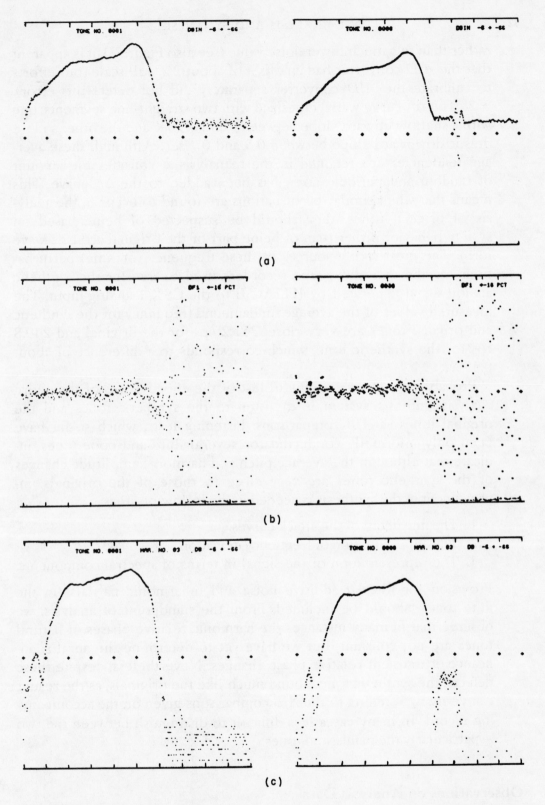

Figure 11. Comparison of the analysis of original and synthetic flute tones ($f = 252$ cps): (a) s_{rms}(db); (b) Δf_1; (c) c_3 (db).

rather than to a much lower noise value (see also Figure 7), it is apparent that the A/D converter had an offset of about 2% full scale (our efforts to calibrate the A/D converter separately did not detect this error).

2. The Δf_1 curve was synthesized with two straight-line segments, one with a shallow upward slope between 0 and 0.5 sec and the other a more drastic downward slope between 0.5 and 0.7 sec. Although these average tendencies are retained in the reanalysis, a considerable amount of random and periodic noise has been added to the Δf_1 curve. This means that when similar perturbations are found to occur in the analysis of original tones, they should be suspected of being based on system behavior rather than of being part of the original acoustic wave form. The most likely sources of these frequency (or time) perturbations are the two audio tape recorders used to transfer the synthetic analog signal generated by ILLIAC II to the CSX-1 analog input. The measured values of the average fundamental frequency for the synthetic and original tones are very close: 251.2 cps for the original and 249.8 cps for the synthetic tone, which corresponds to a difference of about 0.55%.

Probably the most meaningful test of the effectiveness of the entire analysis-synthesis system is to listen to the synthetic tones and the original tones as A/B comparisons. Listening tests, which so far have been only informally conducted for several flute and oboe tones, indicate that although the average pitch and harmonic amplitude changes of the synthetic tones are very close to those of the originals improvement in the synthesis is needed in the following areas:

1. The fine detail of the attack curves.
2. The approximation of frequency deviation.
3. The representation of the signal in terms of spectral components.

Provision for filtered additive noise and inharmonic partials (in the flute tones) should be included. From the standpoint of analysis, we observe that in many instances the harmonic relative phases of natural tones are not constant, but we have yet to determine the aural significance of transient relative phase changes. Nevertheless, despite these defects, the synthetic tones sound much like the originals, as the reader can verify by listening to the A/B comparisons given on the accompanying record. In many cases it is difficult to distinguish between the two — particularly the pianissimo tones.

Observations on Analysis Data

One of the problems present in making generalizations about the behavior of musical instrument tones is that each musician tends to have a number of different playing styles (that is, methods of tongueing and so on) and varies them from tone to tone. Also, different notes on a musical instrument are played by varying the positions of keys (for the wind instruments) or of the bow and particular string (for the string instruments), thus adding to the number of possibilities. These factors help to create variety in musical expression, but they increase the difficulty in categorizing the analyses.

The following observations about the data collected should be considered as preliminary and descriptive in scope because many of our data are yet to be processed. Five of our sources of analysis data are the following:

1. Display graphs.
2. Maximum values of harmonic amplitudes (printed during analysis computation).
3. Printed output of complete data generated by ANMAG.
4. LINSEG output data.
5. "Post-analysis" programs.

Flute (two different players), oboe, violin, cornet, and trumpet tones have been analyzed so far, but for the most part only the flute is treated in this article.

Observations on Display Graphs

The parameters for 36 flute tones by one player (Thomas Howell) produced at fundamental frequencies between 252 and 898 Hz were displayed and photographed. Of general interest are the shapes of the attack curves, the changes in fundamental frequency, and the nature of the deviations (if any) of the relative phases.

The s_{rms} and harmonic amplitude curves are generally distinguished by definite attack, steady state, and decay sections. From the display photographs the attack times for the s_{rms} curves were judged (by this writer) to have values between 50 and 250 msec, whereas a computer program described on p. 60 calculated values ranging from 20 to 445 msec. In neither case does there appear to be any strong correlation between attack time and fundamental frequency, as one investigative team suggests [17], although the attack times for the *mf* and *ff* tones seem, on the average, to decrease with pitch from about 150 msec at 250 Hz to 50 msec at 900 cps. In fact, if certain exceptional tones could be left out of the analysis, some very nice curves could be plotted for both cases!

The amplitude curves for the harmonics were plotted on both linear and logarithmic scales. When we look at the linear versions, we notice that quite frequently the attacks of the higher number harmonics appear to begin at later times than the attack of the first harmonic (fundamental). This effect is most consistently calculated if a straight line is fitted to the most prominent attack segment of each $c_k(t)$ curve and passed through the time axis to determine each value of the onset time. The onset time for $c_2(t)$ minus the onset time for $c_1(t)$ was judged to take on values between 60 and -10 msec; on the average this difference tended to decrease from about 50 msec at $f_1 = 250$ cps to 0 msec at $f_1 = 900$ Hz for the *mf* and *ff* tones but to increase from 10 msec at 350 Hz to 40 msec at 900 Hz for the *pp* tones.

Attack times and onset times are more difficult to judge consistently from the log amplitude plots because an arbitrary threshold amplitude must be chosen whose meaningfulness may vary from tone to tone. However, most attack segments and nearly all decay segments appear as exponential curves on a linear amplitude scale and as straight lines on a log scale. Hence on the linear scale these segments can be characterized by the expression $A \cdot 10^{\alpha(t-t_o)/20}$, where α is the attack or decay rate in decibels per second; α is also the slope of the best fit straight line, as measured on the log scale. Values for α were measured for the first six harmonics for the attack segments of all 36 tones and for the decay segments when possible (some decays were cut off because of the 1 sec duration limit). These values seemed to correlate better when plotted against the frequencies of the corresponding harmonic amplitudes instead of against the fundamental frequencies. The values were plotted on a log-log grid. The attack rates do not appear to correlate at all with intensity, but, when all calculated values are plotted against frequency, we find them randomly distributed within a definite region. Only certain inordinately high attack rates (1200 to 6000 db/sec), which occur for $c_1(t)$ at the lowest frequencies, lie outside this region. The region is contained quite well by a half-ellipse. The end points of the bottom flat edge of the ellipse lie at (300 db/sec, 250 Hz) and (200 db/sec, 500 Hz), and the point of greatest curvature of the ellipse is (1500 db/sec, 1400 Hz). Typical values for attack rates are 50 db/sec for $300 < f_k < 800$ Hz, 60 db/sec for $800 < f_k < 2000$ Hz, and 35 db/sec for $2000 < f_k < 3000$ Hz. The spread of possible values, however, is greatest (from 270 to 1200 db/sec) in the 800 to 2000 Hz region. The decay rates correlate much better with respect to frequency and dynamics. The data for *mf* tones can be approximated fairly well by a parabola passing through the points (250 db/sec, 250 Hz), (750 db/sec, 1200 Hz), and (300 db/sec, 2500 Hz). Corresponding curves for the *ff* and *pp* tones lie above and below this curve, respectively.

Spectral Analysis

It is well known that a close analogy exists between musician-musical instrument coupled systems and the combination of a filter driven by an electrical oscillator. The description of the first type of system is complicated because of the large degree of flexibility in the coupling between the musician and his instrument. This coupling affects the filter characteristics by altering the boundary conditions — this can be treated as a variable source impedance — and the source waveform, which is generated in a fashion analogous to the electrical oscillator. The description is further complicated by the possibility of pressures and vibrations large enough at the inputs to musical instruments to violate the linearity condition in the derivation of the wave equation.

For a first-order analogy, however, we can assign unique and invariant spectral functions to the waveform and filter response. Therefore for the steady state the harmonic amplitudes for a given tone can be expressed by

$$c_k = A\, w_k\, M(kf_a), \tag{31}$$

where A is the input amplification level, w_k is the kth harmonic amplitude of the input (excitation) wave form, and $M(f)$ is the filter response function, including the room frequency response.

The harmonic amplitudes may also be expressed in terms of a continuous spectral envelope function of frequency:

$$c(f) = Aw\left(\frac{f}{f_a}\right)M(f), \qquad f_a \le f \le n_h f_a, \tag{32}$$

where $c(f)$ interpolates the values c_k, $k = 1, \ldots, n_h$.

Continuous spectral envelopes for many tones of several musical instruments have been constructed by connecting the points representing the discrete spectra with straight lines. Each vertical coordinate is the maximum value of a harmonic amplitude over a one-sec interval. The envelopes for a given instrument played at one dynamic level (pp, mf, or ff) are combined in one graph by using logarithmic scales for both frequency and amplitude. Figures 12a, b, and c show the combined curves for the flute, violin, and oboe, respectively, at mf.

These combined envelopes — or, more accurately, the points connected by the straight lines — describe a statistical spectrum space characteristic of the musical instrument at the given dynamic level. For all instruments studied so far the difference between the spectrum spaces for pp and mf is much greater than that between the mf and ff spaces.

Assuming that w is nearly independent of frequency, that M describes a smooth curve, and A changes more or less randomly from one

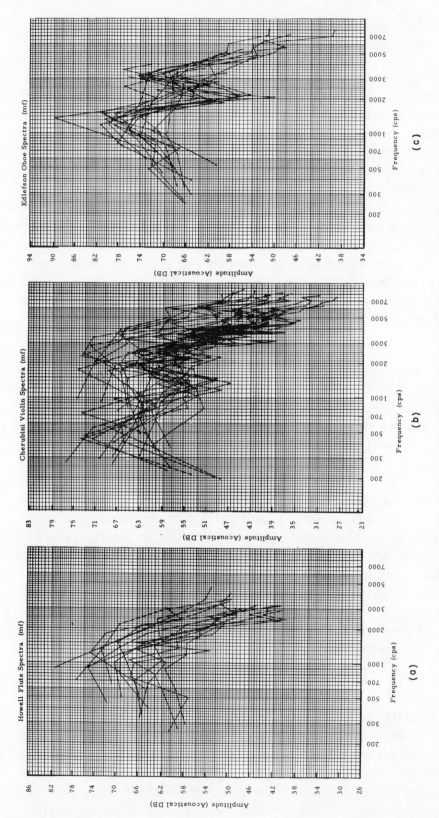

Figure 12. Combined spectral envelopes for (a) flute, (b) violin, and (c) oboe.

56

mf tone to the next, we can attempt to reveal the shape of M by moving the individual spectral envelopes up and down to minimize the deviation from an "apparent" curve. This method has been used by Luce (10), and the result with our data for the oboe tones at *mf* is shown in Figure 13*a*. It should be noted that if w is a function of f, rather than f/f_a, this curve represents $w(f) M(f)$ within a scale factor, rather than $M(f)$ alone. On the other hand, if w is a function of f/f_a, it would be possible to achieve only a reasonable deviation if $w(f/f_a)$ and $M(f)$ were strictly linear on the log-log graph.

In another scheme for investigating spectral characteristics we assume that for a given dynamic level A is independent of f_a and w is a function of f/f_a. If this assumption is correct and we plot c_1 versus f_a, c_2 versus $2f_a, \ldots$, and c_{n_h} versus $n_h f_a$ on separate graphs, each plot should trace a portion of the curve for $M(f)$. This is true because each plot would correspond to the output of a filter driven by a constant amplitude sine wave. Since the frequency regions for each curve overlap, the total curve for $M(f)$ can be constructed by fitting the individual sections together by the method of altering the vertical positions of each graph. Altering the vertical position on a log scale is equivalent to multiplying the vertical coordinates by a fixed factor for each harmonic. The set of alignment factors ordered according to harmonic number then gives the spectrum of the input waveform. The results of this treatment of the data for the cornet tones at *pp* and *mf* dynamic levels are given in Figures 13*b* and *c*, respectively. The high-pass frequency response, which is known to be characteristic of the horn, shows up in the *mf* graph. The *ff* plot is almost identical to it, but the *pp* plot that follows it for low frequencies shows a rapid cutoff at high frequencies. This is probably a result of the dependence of w, the excitation wave shape, directly on f_a.

In any case it is difficult to justify that the separation of the excitation from the filter responses according to these two methods really corresponds to the actual physical behavior of the instruments analyzed. It can only be said at this time that the spectrum spaces represented by Figure 12 represent accurate data and that the given curves may be useful for simulating steady-state timbres of musical instruments. A more rigorous analysis of musical instruments should include a separate measurement of the excitation functions synchronously with the output signals.

Nonlinear Analysis

Even though it has been obvious for some time that musical instru-

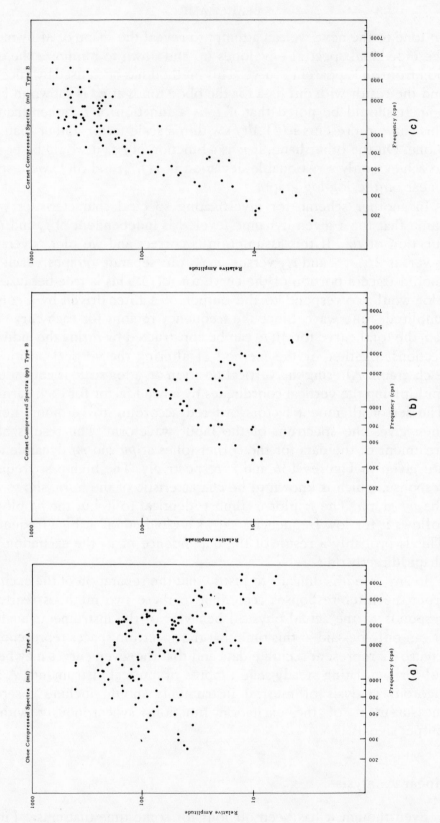

Figure 13. Compressed spectra envelopes for (a) oboe, (b) cornet, and (c) cornet.

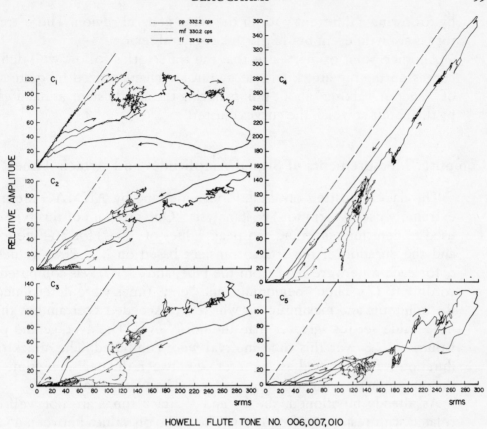

HOWELL FLUTE TONE NO. 006,007,010

Figure 14. Harmonic amplitudes of flute tones plotted against the total rms signal amplitude at three different dynamic levels with time as a parameter. Arrows show direction of increasing time.

ments are characterized by their frequency or "formant" characteristics, it has also become evident recently that the changes in spectrum for constant pitch may be strongly correlated with intensity. Risset [8] has studied this effect in trumpet tones. Figure 14 shows the comparison of the behaviors of the harmonic amplitudes of flute tones played at the same pitch but at three different dynamic levels, *pp, mf,* and *ff*. These plots appear as "trajectories," since, for each harmonic k, c_k is plotted against s_{rms} with time as the parameter. The plots are interesting because they clearly show in an "amplitude space" the dependence of the individual c_k's on s_{rms}, regardless of actual amplitudes. However the correspondence is not definitely one-to-one; for example, the c_1 versus s_{rms} trajectory traces an almost linear curve for dynamic *pp*, for in this case the tone is almost purely sinusoid. For dynamic *mf* the trajectory traces this curve for an instant during the attack and then breaks to the right along a new trajectory; it returns to the origin during the decay by following a different path in the same general region. The *ff* trajectory is again different but in the same general region.

Another point of interest is that the trajectories follow well-defined curves during the attack and decay but are characterized by quite a bit of "random walking" about points during the steady state, as manifested by the points at which the curves cluster.

Computer Measurements of Signal Amplitudes and Attack Times

The data as written on digital magnetic tape by ANMAG are in an extremely useful form for "postanalysis." One program of this type was used to determine average and peak values of $s_{rms}(t)$ for 36 flute tones and the duration of the attack transient based on $\tilde{s}_{rms}$. First, values of c_k for each tone were read from the tape, and $\tilde{s}_{rms}(t)$ was computed according to (7). Then "beginning" and "end" times were determined as the minimum and maximum for which $\tilde{s}_{rms}$ exceeded a certain low threshold value set just greater than the noise level. The average and peak values of s_{rms} over this time interval were computed. The attack time duration was computed as the interval between the beginning time and the minimum time for which s_{rms} exceeded its average value.

As already mentioned, the *mf* and *ff* attack times are not well correlated with respect to frequency. They take on values between 45 and 445 msec. However, *pp* attack times take on values between 20 and 45 msec and, perhaps coincidentally, fall on a smooth curve with maxima at 350 and 800 cps and a minimum at 500 cps. The values of peak rms and average rms amplitude versus frequency for each dynamic level fluctuate about average lines that show an increase with frequency at a rate of approximately 6 db/octave. The average difference in levels between *ff* and *mf* is about 3 db, whereas the difference between *mf* and *pp* is about 8 db. The general increase in amplitude with pitch can be attributed to the necessity for higher velocities of breath in order to achieve the higher frequency edge tones at the embouchure of the flute.

ACKNOWLEDGEMENTS

I should like to extend my sincere thanks to James P. Fornango, who wrote the analysis and display programs, and to Gary R. Grossman, who wrote the synthesis and D/A conversion programs. Their contributions were extremely valuable and, indeed, indispensable, considering our time schedule. I should also like to thank Drs. H. Eugene Slottow and Richard Jenks of the Coordinated Science Laboratory and Mr. Cliff

Carter of the Digital Computer Laboratory for their cooperation in allowing the use of computers for this special experiment. The investigation was supported by the National Science Foundation and the Magnavox Company.

REFERENCES

[1] G. S. Ohm, Ueber die Definition des Tones, nebst daren geknüpfter Theorie der Sirene und ahnlicher tonbildender Vorrichtungen, *Ann. Phys. Chem.*, **59**, 513–565 (1843).

[2] H. L. F. Von Helmholtz, (translated by A. J. Ellis), *On the Sensation of Tone as a Physiological Basis for the Theory of Music,* Dover, New York (1954).

[3] R. Plomp, The Ear as a Frequency Analyzer, *J. Acoust. Soc. Am.,* **36** (9), 1628–1636 (1964).

[4] H. Fletcher, The Pitch, Loudness and Quality of Musical Tones, *Bell Telephone System Monograph No. 1397* (1946).

[5] L. J. Silvian, H. K. Dunn, and S. D. White, Absolute Amplitude and Spectra of Certain Musical Instruments and Orchestras, *Bell Telephone System Monograph No. 3381* (1959).

[6] H. Fletcher, E. D. Blackhorn, and O. N. Geerster, Quality of Violin, Cello, and Bass-Viol Tones, I, *J. Acoust. Soc. Am.,* **37** (5), 851 (1965).

[7] M. D. Freedman, Analysis of Musical Instrument Tones, *J. Acoust. Soc. Am.,* **41** (4), 793–806 (1967).

[8] J. C. Risset, Computer Study of Trumpet Tones, *Bell Telephone Laboratories Internal Report,* Murray Hill, N. J. (1966).

[9] M. V. Mathews, J. E. Miller, J. R. Pierce, and J. Tenney, Computer Study of Violin Tones, *Bell Telephone Laboratories Internal Report,* Murray Hill, N. J. (1966).

[10] D. A. Luce, *Physical Correlates of Non-Percussive Musical Instrument Tones,* Doctoral Thesis, M.I.T., Cambridge, Mass. (1963).

[11] E. E. David, Jr., Digital Simulation in Perceptual Research, *Bell Telephone System Monograph No. 3405-1* (1958).

[12] M. V. Mathews, An Acoustical Compiler for Music and Psychological Stimuli, *Bell System Tech. J.,* **40,** 377 (1961).

[13] M. E. Clark, Jr., et al., Preliminary Experiments on the Aural Significance of Parts of Tones of Orchestral Instruments and on Choral Tones, *J. Audio Eng. Soc.,* **11** (1), 45–54 (1963).

[14] J. W. Beauchamp, *Electronic Instrumentation for the Synthesis, Control, and Analysis of Harmonic Musical Tones,* Doctoral Thesis, University of Illinois, Urbana (1965), Chapter 5.

[15] C. M. Rader and B. Gold, Digital Filter Design Techniques in the Frequency Domain, *Proc. IEEE,* **55** (2), 149–171 (1967).

[16] A. B. Otis, Jr., *An Analog Input-Output System for the ILLIAC II,* M. S. Thesis, University of Illinois, Urbana (1967).

[17] D. A. Luce and M. E. Clark, Durations of Attack Transients of Non-Percussive Orchestral Instruments, *J. Audio Eng. Soc.,* **13** (3), 194–199 (1965).

[18] A. Wood, *The Physics of Music,* Methuen, London (1944), pp. 116–121, 136–140.

Example

> *Musical Instrument Tones*
> *Synthetic versus Real*
> Side 8, Bands 1,2,3
>
> The examples consist of a series of comparisons between some musical tones as they were originally recorded in a sound chamber and the corresponding tones synthesized by a digital computer. The synthetic tones were created by approximating the time graphs of the fundamental frequency and the harmonic amplitudes, as obtained from the analyses of the original tone, with piecewise linear functions. The slight differences between each corresponding synthetic and real tone should be attributable to smoothing and omission of the phase data. The synthetic tones were produced by
>
> The CSX-1 computer (A/D conversion).
> A CDC 1604 computer (analysis).
> An IBM 7094 (tape conversion).
> The Illiac II computer (*D/A* conversion).
>
> Three musical instruments were synthesized: the flute, oboe, and cornet.

Some New Developments in Computer-generated Music

ARTHUR ROBERTS

Argonne National Laboratory
Argonne, Illinois

This article briefly describes the present status of the FORTRAN program ORPHEUS, formerly called MUSIC4F [1]. New features are continually being added to any computer program in active use, and the divergences between ORPHEUS and its parent program MUSIC4 [2] have now reached the point at which a new name seems justified. In particular, ORPHEUS has abandoned the concept of "instruments" assembled by the program each time it runs (although the nomenclature still survives). In effect, there is only one instrument; it contains all the resources of the program and is available to all the individual voices at all times. It is the continued elaboration of the resources of this instrument that we describe here and some of the ways in which they have been used to date. The current version of the program is called ORPHEUS 67A.

NEW FEATURES IN ORPHEUS 67

The major additions that have been made to ORPHEUS since version 65 B of MUSIC4F are the following:

1. Subroutine SYNTH now provides storage for 20 different waveforms. One cycle of each is stored as 250 samples, and each waveform is calculated from the Fourier component partials supplied by the user, the lowest frequency partial being taken as the fundamental. Waveform code 9J calls stored waveform number J.

In addition, the waveform code 10J now uses the same Fourier component data to synthesize the waveform as it is used. If the partials are harmonic, this yields the same result as the stored waveform; if not, an

63

aperiodic waveform can be synthesized to add an entirely new dimension to the kind of sounds available, which occur in enormous variety. These sounds, with suitable envelope treatment, constitute one of the main present resources of the program.

2. The possibility of frequency- or amplitude-modulating any basic waveform has been added in which the modulating signal may contain up to three independent components, each with its own frequency, waveform, and amplitude. Some rather extraordinary sounds can now be obtained in this way.

3. A new OP code, symbolized by HLD, has been added. Notes written with this code are held past the end of a section into succeeding sections, as specified by their duration. This allows long sustained notes, such as organpoints, without exceeding the allowable maximum number of cards in a section (500). Previously there was no way of doing this. Another new code, SPT, allows modifications of the program parameters during the third pass, which is the actual sound generation.

4. A new subroutine, PLF2, with a modified starting time and amplitude specified on the PLF2 card, will play a series of stored notes. This is useful for repeated figures. Another, TSET, changes print-out parameters during execution to facilitate debugging. PASS3 and PLAYER1, having grown too large and complex, have both been split into several shorter subroutines. The waveform-generating function formerly in LOCAL801 is now a separate subroutine OSCIL, which thus becomes available for waveform generation for purposes other than the basic waveform.

EXPERIMENTS ON TIMBRE

One of the besetting faults of electronic sound generation is the difficulty of producing satisfactory sustained tones. A long note (say 2 sec or more) of strictly periodic waveform often sounds "electronic." A periodic vibrato or tremolo does not always cure the trouble, though it may help. Even some aperiodic waveforms, if the aperiodicity is simple enough, may have this difficulty. What is needed is a departure from a constant stimulus, which appears to fatigue the ear.* For this purpose any of the following may suffice:

1. Control of the envelope: crescendo, diminuendo, exponential decay, and so on.

2. Variation of the pitch — vibrato or glissando. Vibrato is better if it is nonuniform.

*Similar phenomena arise in the stimulation of other senses; for example, the visual.

3. Variation of waveform. This is the most interesting and most widely applicable. A continuous variation of harmonic content can be achieved by mixing two or more waveforms in timevarying proportion (e.g., decreasing the sawtooth and raising the squarewave) or by using sufficiently complex aperiodic waveforms.

Short notes do not need this treatment.

NONLINEAR EFFECTS

Another feature of electronic tone that the listener finds distressing, or at least unnatural, is that quality is independent of loudness. Such independence is characteristic of perfectly linear oscillators, and electronic or computer-simulated oscillators are indeed perfectly linear. Consequently, it is impossible to distinguish between a note played softly on the instrument, but sounding loud because the amplifier gain is turned up, and a note played loud, but with lower amplifier gain. This ambiguity seems to carry some psychological distress with it. The cause is probably that we do not have the same emotional response to a loud note as to a soft one and are therefore uncertain which response is appropriate. No such ambiguity occurs in listening to loudspeaker reproductions of most conventional instruments; their nonlinear characteristics are sufficiently marked that we rarely doubt whether the original sound of the instrument was loud or soft, no matter what the volume the reproduction.

It is, of course, easy to correct this feature by introducing deliberate nonlinearities into the computer-simulated oscillators. Some experiments have been made along this line with encouraging but not conclusive results. We may speculate that a certain degree of familiarity with the amplitude-sensitive tone colors may be necessary before a confident judgment about inherent loudness becomes possible and that this implies an invariant loudness-tone quality relation. One of the important degrees of freedom of electronic music is continuously varying tone-color, so that we find ourselves in a quandary: how do we maintain inherent loudness information in the sound and still retain the variable tone-color? In some cases the loudness information may be conveyed by other means, such as transient effects.

AMBIGUOUS SOUNDS

A word of warning is in order concerning sounds to which the ear is already trained to give an alternative interpretation. This applies not only to sounds resembling familiar ones—such as telephone bells or gunshots—but also to less-obvious circumstances. Thus there is a passage in the second movement of the *Sonatina* (see below) in which a conventional waveform is gradually transformed to a rectangular wave (by the process of respective fading out and in). It nearly always elicits a negative audience reaction and electronically adept listeners will warn me that the amplifier is overloaded and clipping. This impression is enhanced if there is also a crescendo.

Many experiments have been done with combinations of enharmonic partials. Slight detuning produces beats. A strong enharmonic partial dividing the interval between harmonic partial into commensurable fractions will simply shift the fundamental. Thus, for example, given the sequence of partials $3f, 4f, 5f, 6f$, which yield the fundamental f, the addition of $3.5f$ or $4.5f$ shifts the fundamental to $0.5f$, and $3.33f$ to $f/3$. Depending on its intensity and pitch, a single incommensurable partial may simply alter the timbre or produce the impression of a chord with several distinct frequencies. Incommensurable closely spaced frequencies give a drumlike quality in the low register (with the appropriate envelope).

Gradual, uniform timbre changes, produced by mixing different waveforms in time-varying proportions, have a strong expressive effect like that of a crescendo or diminuendo. So also has a vibrato in the range of 15 to 30 cps.

ACKNOWLEDGMENT

This work has been supported by the Applied Mathematics Division. I should like particularly to mention the assistance and encouragement of W. Givens and C. G. LeVee.

REFERENCES

[1] A. Roberts, *Audio Eng. Soc.*, **14**, 17 *(1966)*.
[2] M. V. Mathews, *Bell System Tech. J.*, **40**, 677 *(1961)*. M. V. Mathews, and Joan E. Miller, *MUSIC4 Programmer's Manual* (Bell Telephone Laboratories, Murray Hill, N. J., unpublished).
[3] *LINK*, 16mm color sound film. Further information is available from Film Center, Tech. Public. Dept., Argonne National Laboratory, Argonne, Ill.

Examples

1. *Sonatina for CDC-3600*
Side 2, Bands 1,2,3

This exercise in computer operation is in three movements. The first, a scherzo, uses only pitches of the tempered scale and an early, somewhat restricted palette of tone colors. Its chief aim is an investigation of some of the possibilities afforded by the computer of rapid complex multivoice passages.

The second movement is an exercise in quarter- and eighth-tone notes, in which particular attention is given to chromatic passages. The computer is an ideal medium for exploring such microintervals; being tone-deaf, it never plays out of tune. The pronounced tendency of the ear to hear a chromatic progression as a succession of half-tones, even when they are eighth- or quarter-tones, is noteworthy. We have already mentioned the tendency of the ear to interpret the change in tone quality at the climax as amplifier overloading (it is not, although it simulates it very well by fading into a rectangular waveform that approximates the clipping produced by a heavy overload).

The last movement, a short rondo, explores two further dimensions: perfectly free pitches not connected to any scale, and an assortment of aperiodic waveforms, mostly with percussionlike envelopes. It turns out to be easy to simulate drum sounds by using only a few (three to five) unrelated Fourier components in a narrow frequency span (say a 2.5–1 ratio). Again, with free pitches, the ear vigorously attempts to associate them with scale pitches. The rondo also includes an attempt to explore the potential humor in the odd noises available.

2. *Title Music to LINK*
    Side 2, Band 4

This short excerpt is the background music for the title and screen credits for the short documentary film *LINK* produced by the Argonne National Laboratory film group [3]. The film explains the operation of a computer program LINK, written by R. K. Clark of the Applied Mathematics Division at Argonne, for use in the automatic analysis of spark chamber photographs taken during experiments in high energy physics. Since it concerns a CDC-3600 computer program and includes computer-produced animation sequences which were photographed directly from the computer cathode-ray-tube display and which illustrate the program operation, it seemed only appropriate for the computer to provide the music with which to accompany and emphasize its accomplishments. Though the selection is only a minute long, it is in fact quite complex, accurately synchronized to the film (synchronization is a trivial problem) and contains some noteworthy illustrative effects.

3. *Rocket*
   Side 8, Band 4

This little etude is a study in long sustained notes to overcome their tendency to sound "electronic" by introducing suitable variety. It also demonstrates another feature of the electronic medium, although not to its full capacity — the very wide dynamic range, rivaled only by the full orchestra and the organ.

II

Algorithms in Composition

If we are given the general form of the way in which a proposition is constructed, then thereby we are also given the general form of the way in which by an operation out of one proposition another can be created.

WITTGENSTEIN: *Tractatus:* 6.002

Some Compositional Techniques Involving the Use of Computers

LEJAREN HILLER

University of Illinois
Urbana, Illinois

In 1963 Robert Baker and I set up a compositional programming language called MUSICOMP which provides, either within itself or in conjunction with standard programming languages such as SCATRE and FORTRAN, basic techniques for generating original musical scores. The first and admittedly not particularly refined exploitation of this language is embodied in our *Computer Cantata,* a composition based primarily on stochastic choice processes. A disk recording of a performance of this composition and of the earlier *Illiac Suite for String Quartet* has recently been released [1]. In addition, rather complete descriptions of the *Computer Cantata* have been printed [2, 3] and the score of the work is expected to be published soon [4].

In the present article I plan, first, to review briefly what we have done since 1963 and, second, to provide a more detailed discussion of a new composition now being completed, namely, *Algorithms I and II.* Although this work is not yet done, there is enough of it finished so that recently we were able to record a trial version of its first half with the University of Illinois Contemporary Chamber Players. Consequently I propose to discuss the first half of this piece and, in particular, one movement of it in some detail. A recording of this particular movement is included as an illustration of one kind of result that can be obtained by programming selected compositional processes for a computer.

Let me turn briefly to chronology. Since 1963 we have written a programming manual for MUSICOMP, a revised version of which was recently issued as a technical report from our Experimental Music Studio [5]. In line with the philosophy we employed in designing MUSICOMP, this is a loose-leaf manual that permits the insertion of new programs as they are written and checked out and the deletion of older programs that become obsolete. In effect, then, MUSICOMP is not a fixed entity but an adaptable language that we expect to change and to expand as our programming experience mounts.

We have divided the source decks into three basic parts: "System Regulatory Routines," "Compositional and Analytical Subroutines," and "Sound Synthesis Routines." The last are not actual synthesis programs but rather routines that prepare and organize data that serve as input to sound-generating programs described elsewhere [6, 7].

One essential feature of MUSICOMP, then, has to do with the writing of subroutines that accomplish specific compositional tasks. The subroutines already written up in generalized format and already included in, or shortly to be added to the MUSICOMP manual are shown in Table 1.

Table 1 lists only those subroutines that have been thoroughly checked out, annotated, and, in most instances, written up for inclusion in the MUSICOMP programming manual. In addition, there now exist programs that have not yet been converted into closed subroutines but are nevertheless operational. Among them are programs that accomplish the following:

Table 1.
Currently Available MUSICOMP Subroutines

System Library Subroutines

1.	LOAD	(establishment of addresses required for use of the MUSICOMP choice order code)
2.	EXECUT	(establishment of a provisional format specification)
3.	ACTION	(execution of the MUSICOMP choice order code and storage of the results)
4.	PRUNIT	(special decimal print out for code-checking)
5.	FORMAT	(specifications of limitations on choices and symbolic representation of printout)
6.	FINISH	(termination of program)
7.	FINT-S	(simple printout routine from SCATRE programs)
8.	FINT-F	(simple printout routine from FORTRAN programs)
9.	UPRINT	(simple printout routine from one type of storage format)

Compositional Subroutines

1.	ML.DST	(single choice of an integer according to a stored probability distribution)

Table 1 (*continued*)

2.	ML2DST	(single choice of an integer according to a stored probability distribution with probabilities normalized to 1)
3.	ML3DST	(single choice of an integer according to a random probability distribution)
4.	ML4DST	(stochastic choice of a set of rhythmic durations)
5.	ML.ZPF	(single choice of an integer according to Zipf's law for distribution)
6.	ML.PCH	(stochastic choice of a range of pitches and then of a specific pitch from this range)
7.	ML.MOD	(choice of a rhythmic mode)
8.	ML.SUM	(summation of rhythmic choices for control of a rhythmic plan)
9.	ML.ROW	(extraction of an element of a stored row)
10.	SHUFFL	(random shuffle of a number of items on a list)
11.	XTRACT	(extraction of a previous choice from stored choices of a score already composed)
12.	MATCH	(ordering of durations in a "line B" to make the best possible match to a sequence of durations in a "line A")
13.	ORD.0	(zeroth-order stochastic process; all choices equiprobable)
14.	ORD.1	(first-order stochastic process; a choice according to a fixed-frequency distribution)
15.	ORD.2	(second-order stochastic process; a choice dependent on the previous choice)
16.	ORD.3	(third-order stochastic process; a choice dependent on the difference between the two previous choices)
17.	ORD.4	(fourth-order stochastic process; a choice dependent on the difference between the differences between the previous three choices)
18.	ORD.5	(fifth-order stochastic process; a choice dependent on the difference between the differences between the differences between the previous four choices)
19.	ORD.6	(sixth-order stochastic process; a choice dependent on the difference between the differences between the differences between the differences between the previous five choices)
20.	S.D.C.	(computation of all possible sums and differences followed by a random choice of one of the values so computed)
21.	ML.CDC	(computation of a dissonance-consonance index)
22.	ML.RL1	(a skip-stepwise rule; in a single line a large melodic skip must be followed by a small one)
23.	ML.RL2	(melodic range rule; in a single line a limit such as an octave is imposed on melodic motion)
24.	ML.RL3	(resolution rule: vertical intervals such as tritones and sevenths are resolved inwardly or outwardly; operational for up to 12 parallel lines)

Sound Synthesis Subroutines

1.	CSX-1	(sound output for the CSX-1 "Music Machine")
2.	DIGAN1	(simplest sound output routine for ILLIAC II-*D/A* sound synthesis)
3.	DIGAN2	(modified sound output routine for ILLIAC II-*D/A* sound synthesis)
4.	DIGAN3	(modified sound output routine for DIGAN2 for FORTRAN programs)
5.	INTRFC	(routine for putting sound output data on digital tape for loading on ILLIAC II)
6.	TINIT TTERM1 TTERM2	(routines used in conjunction with INTRFC for digital tape control and data format storage design)

1. Control of the choice of stochastic order according to an imposed probability distribution used in conjunction with subroutines ORD.0 through ORD.6. It is a closed subroutine called DIST and is now being slightly rewritten to generalize it.

2. Generation of a frequency distribution. This is a FORTRAN program that computes distributions from standard equations for such distributions.

3. Generation of phrases and their imitations and permutations. This is a FORTRAN routine that generates and labels groups of notes and permits them to be used as fundamental components in larger structures.

4. Generation of all the permutations of a given row of n items.

5. Generation of similar rhythmic data for more than one instrument for any length of time. This permits instruments to double one another rhythmically and to regroup whenever desired.

6. Generation of dynamics indications and playing styles according to serial processes.

7. Reading in of musical phrases for computer processing. This program is useful for analytical as well as compositional work.

8. A control routine that permits all programs to be used in structures where rhythmic durations are irregular. This permits such things as delayed resolutions, anticipations, and so on.

9. A program written by Bernard Waxman, one of our graduate assistants and me which provides a generalized solution of the problem of "change ringing," a permutational method of composition that developed over the centuries in connection with the ringing of church bells. Papworth [8] recently programmed for a computer one special system of change ringing. His example provided us the stimulus to write a generalized analysis and generation program for our own use.

Obviously the more subroutines we have, the more subtle and varied we can make our musical compositions. Needless to say, the number of subroutines we have in our programming library is limited by the willingness of composers to sit down and write them and get them running properly.

I believe the purposes of the subroutines listed in Table 1 are obvious in most instances. Even so, let us examine one of them in more detail. ML.ROW, for example, permits us to extract any pitch from any transposition of any one of the four forms—original, inversion, retrograde, or retrograde inversion—of a row such as a 12-tone row. By setting up appropriate logical loops and entries into this subroutine, we are able to handle one important component process of serial composition directly. Figure 1 shows the use of this subroutine in more detail. The three parameters I, F, and J must, in the actual calling sequence, be replaced by specific integers that represent the element of the row, the transposition of the row, and the form of the row, respectively. The calling sequence shown provides an explicit example of how this is done.

ALGORITHMS I AND II—
A NEW COMPUTER MUSIC COMPOSITION

To illustrate and clarify my ideas, I believe it might be profitable next to examine some of the programming that I am currently employing in writing a new composition entitled *Algorithms I and II.* Actually, this is a twin composition made up of *Algorithms I,* which is now virtually complete, and *Algorithms II,* which will be finished during the coming year. Although it is not unlikely that I may make some changes in the projected details of *Algorithms II,* the total plan is now fixed as follows:

Algorithms I
I.   The Decay of Information
II. Icosahedron
III. Incorporations
Algorithms II
IV. Refinements
V.   Change Ringing
VI. Synthesis

```
             MUSICOMP:  USE OF ML.ROW

           LOCATION     OPERATION     VARIABLE FIELD
Calling    P            Call          ML.ROW,R,...,n

Sequence:               PZE           i,f,j

Return     P+3

    R is the first location of a list of n items.
    f is the form of the row sought.
    j is the transposition sought.
    i is the ordinal number of the item sought.

    Example:  If n=12, i=11, f=2, j=7 we obtain the
              11th note of the retrograde version of
              a 12-tone row transposed upwards a perfect
              fifth.

              So we write in the program
              !!!!!
              CALL     ML.ROW,R,..., 12
              PZE      11, 2, 7
              !!!!!
```

Figure 1.   Use of ML.ROW as an example of actual programming.

Moreover, each movement will exist in four "versions," any one of which can be chosen for a given performance, and each will reflect small but important changes in the parameters that have been inserted into the various compositional subroutines. Consequently the changes will serve not only to demonstrate that they can drastically alter the over-all effect of a given general musical structure but also will permit the controlled and identified isolation of the specific effect of a particular musical parameter on the impression of the whole. This is a novel application of a standard type of experimental design.

All four "versions" of *Algorithms I* should be completed by the end of October 1968. The remaining work principally entails the thorough checking out of a few remaining routines, the transcription of results, and the synthesis of two lines of sound for audio tapes. The piece is scored for flute, clarinet, bassoon, trumpet, harp, tape recorder, percussion, violin, cello, and double bass.

Let me now describe each movement rather briefly in general terms and also present a somewhat more detailed examination of the second movement so that I can illustrate more precisely how some of our programming is carried out.

The first movement, "The Decay of Information," is a short introductory piece that recapitulates in condensed form the formal structure of the *Computer Cantata*. It is based on an evolving plan of stochastic control in which transition probabilities are allowed to increase in complexity from the zeroth to the sixth order. These transition probabilities are not the same at any time for the various instruments, since some instruments reach a sixth-order level of control sooner than others. In fact, a skewed statistical profile controls this particular development. In addition, we have used Zipf's law to select pitches, intervals, differences of intervals, and so on. You may recall that Zipf's law states that the occurrence of a symbol in any language, including music, bears an inverse relationship to the rank order of the symbol. Finally, we specified that the information level of this movement should drop from 100 to 50% from its beginning to its end; hence the title. In this connection let me note that further details regarding this movement have recently been published [9]. These remarks were made in a talk I gave early in 1966 when I was starting work on *Algorithms I*. Although they are still essentially correct, a considerable number of small differences in details of programming have since been made. They will be the subject of a future publication.

"Icosahedron," the second movement, is my first extended effort at programming a reasonably complex serial composition. The title is taken from the name of the geometrical object with 12 apices and 20 faces of three and five sides arranged symmetrically in three dimensions around a focal point. This geometrical object suggested the use of arrangements of three and five units as well as 12 to be combined in various ways in the whole.

The movement consists of 576 notes made up of a row, its three permutations, and the 11 transpositions of these four fundamental forms. Thus each variant of the row occurs once and just once. The row, the sequence of its variants, the dynamics plan, and all rhythmic units are chosen by random number processes. The whole assembly of note occurrences is compiled into a triangular plan, as shown in Figure 2. The 12 "voices" do not correspond, by the way, in a one-to-one relationship to the actual instrumentation. Simultaneities of rhythmic events maximized at the center of the composition were accomplished by means of the subroutine "Match," listed in Table 1. It might be interesting to examine this routine in more detail, since a trial version of this movement is included on the illustrative record accompanying this book.

Match accepts two sequences of numbers that represent rhythmic durations of any pattern from completely random to highly organized. It then matches line B against line A to line up equivalent rhythmic durations as they would occur in time. Because of the way tag bits are employed in the storage of the rhythmic data in this particular routine, Match can enter either voice at any designated point, such as the beginning, the middle, or the end, and can run the matching process forward, backward, or both ways. In the present instance, I choose the centers of the voices as the entry points and match in both directions to follow the structural plan outlined above.

Match then puts the designated first note of list A into a reference location and searches down list B for an identical value. If this value is found, it is moved to the top of list B. This is a direct one-to-one match, and when it occurs the routine is advanced one step to examine the next

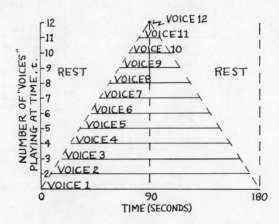

Figure 2. Structural plan of the second movement of *Algorithms I*.

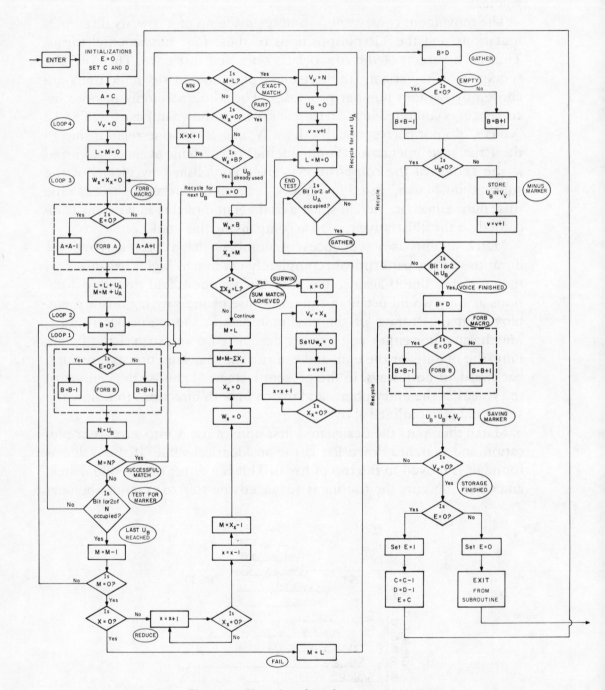

Figure 3. Flow chart for subroutine "MATCH."

note in list A. If such a note is not found, the value of the note in list A is reduced by one and the process is repeated. This is continued until the first largest rhythmic duration smaller than the note in list A is found and moved into a temporary storage location. Match then seeks to fill out the rest of the duration given in list A. If a successful match of these rhythmic subdivisions of the note in list A is found from list B, these values are moved ahead in list B. However, if no such match is found, the next note in list A is added to the one already tested and we start over again, this time trying to match against the enlarged duration in list A. This process continues until either all of list B or list A is used up and successfully matched or until failure occurs. In the latter case, the more usual one, the remaining items on each list are collected and added to the successful matches without further treatment. Figure 3 shows the flow chart from Match to illustrate how this rather complex operation is achieved. Table 2 shows a small example of how the routine works — two rhythmic sequences actually generated for "Icosahedron" before and after "Match" was used on them.

Table 2.

Rhythmic Matching by Subroutine "Match"

List B (Before)	List A (Reference)	List B (After)
1	23	21
9	2	2
25	16	2
21	2	15
17	10	1
2	4	11
10	15	1
7	7	19
48	8	7
6	20	8
8	14	20
17	18	32
21	6	6
1	11	17
6	6	10
3	11	9
78	3	3
20	8	48
19	8	17
32	39	6
7	27	6
2	3	25
6	27	Unmatched	21
11	27	78
15	12	7

Table 3.

The Four "Versions" of Icosahedron

Version	Pitch Row	Maximum Melodic Interval	Playing Style Variations	Rhythmic Choices	Dynamics and Playing Style Rows	DIGAN1 or DIGAN2
I	1	Octave	Limited	Set 1	2	1
II	2	Tritone	Limited	Set 2	1	1
III	1	Tritone	Extensive	Set 1	1	2
IV	2	Octave	Extensive	Set 2	2	2

Table 3 lists the differences between the four versions of this movement. Row 2 is obtained by inserting an extra entry into SHUFFL, and the maximum size of melodic skips is set by one single instruction (a CAS instruction in SCATRE). DIGAN1 and DIGAN2 are two of the sound synthesis routines listed in Table 1. Finally, the second original set of rhythms was obtained by programming 553 waste entries into a random number generator as a special initialization routine.

As I mentioned earlier, a performance of a "trial version" of this movement is contained in the samples on the disk recording accompanying this book. This trial version is more or less a composite of the versions listed in Table 3. It makes use of Row 1, a tritone limit on melodic skips, a limited number of choices of playing styles (e.g., only *arco* on strings), the first set of rhythmic choices, and DIGAN1.

The third movement, "Incorporations," is a sort of rondo form in which I now seek to add to the basic stochastic generators of the first movement a number of modifying processes suggested by more-or-less familiar processes of composition. The structure of this movement is shown in Table 4. As you can see, I was interested in writing a number of useful subroutines that may be employed whenever we wish to modify or refine a stochastic matrix. It is subroutines like these that provide structural flux in a composition primarily dependent on the more generalized and slow moving statistical patterns of stochastic music. Many of these rules represent newly written programs derived from earlier experiments but now written in our new MUSICOMP language or in SCATRE or FORTRAN, both of which are compatible with MUSICOMP. Briefly, the chord evaluation process is based on the computation of the ratio of the sum of the squares to the square of the sums of all the intervals in any given chord. This is a generalization of a process of evaluating three-note chords used in producing two sections of *Computer Cantata*. The three contrapuntal processes are taken from our earlier experience in writing "Experiment Three" of the *Illiac Suite* but now adapted to any number of voices, not just four. The phrase-generation and imitation subroutine permits us to begin to think of larger units than isolated notes, just as in language there comes a time when words and phrases are more useful to deal with than isolated letters of the alphabet. This, by the way, is one subroutine we found easier to write in FOR-TRAN than in SCATRE.

Next, I thought it desirable to be able to group instruments easily by rhythmic structure—again an extension of some earlier work done with the *Illiac Suite,* which is also true of the short cadence at the end of this movement. Note finally that after each process has been demonstrated in a given chordal section it is incorporated into a statistical matrix as a test of its particular efficacy for control of musical choices.

It is obvious that there are still many other controls, relationships, and correlations that must be considered, and it is the purpose of the second half of *Algorithms I and II* to present routines for some of the more important of them. Since this section of the work is still to be written, I shall be brief about it at this time.

Table 4.

Structural Plan of "Incorporations"[a]

Section	Content	Duration (seconds)	
1A	Sixth-order stochastic music	8	
			48
2A	Chord evaluation in terms of a dissonance-consonance index	40	
1B	Combination of the above with fifth-order stochastic music	16	
			48
2B	Three contrapuntal processes	32	
3A	Combination of the above with fourth-order stochastic process	24	
			48
3B	Phrase generation, imitation, and free transition	24	
4A	Combination of the above with third- and second-order stochastic processes	32	
			48
4B	Process for grouping voices into rhythmic blocks	16	
5A	Combination of the above with first- and zeroth-order stochastic processes	40	
			48
5B	Process for a statistical tonal cadence	8	

[a]All "1" sections *allegro;* all "2" sections *andante*

In the fourth movement I wish to develop more internal relationships between rhythms, playing styles, dynamics, and melodic profiles rather than letting them occur more or less independently. I also want to generate more control of thickness of texture (i.e., rest and play proportions) and of solo versus group contrasts. I particularly want to exploit the phrase-generating routine first written for the third movement. The fifth movement, like the second, will be a kind of interlude and will be an exploitation of the change-ringing routine described earlier.

Finally, the sixth movement will be used to summarize and correlate the results. It will be a short, closed form that I hope will demonstrate that we have made considerable progress in learning how to control some of the more important compositional parameters and that composers can finally begin to employ computers for compositional goals that transcend the merely didactic.

REFERENCES

[1] L. A. Hiller and R. A. Baker, *Computer Cantata* (1963) and L. Hiller and L. M. Isaacson, *Illiac Suite for String Quartet* (1957), performed by H. Hamm, soprano with the University of Illinois Contemporary Players, J. McKenzie, conductor, and the University of Illinois Composition String Quartet. 12″ L.P. Recording: Heliodor H/HS-25053.

[2] L. A. Hiller and R. A. Baker, *Computer Cantata:* An Investigation of Compositional Procedure, *Perspectives of New Music,* **3,** 62 (1964).

[3] L. A. Hiller, Informations theorie und Computer musik, in Vol. 8, *Darmstädter Beiträge zur Neuen Musik,* B. Schott's Söhne, Mainz (1964).

[4] L. A. Hiller and R. A. Baker, *Computer Cantata,* New Music Edition, Theodore Presser Co., Bryn Mawr, Pa. (1967).

[5] L. A. Hiller and A. Leal, Revised MUSICOMP Manual, *University of Illinois Experimental Music Studio Technical Report No. 13,* University of Illinois, Urbana (1966, with supplements to be added).

[6] J. L. Divilbiss, The Real-Time Generation of Music with a Digital Computer, *J. Music Theory,* **18,** 99 (1964).

[7] G. R. Grossman and J. W. Beauchamp, A Provisional Sound Generating Program for the ILLIAC II Computer and *D/A* Converter, *University of Illinois Experimental Music Studio Technical Report No. 14,* University of Illinois, Urbana (1966).

[8] D. A. Papworth, Computers and Change Ringing, *The Computer Journal,* **3,** 47 (1960).

[9] L. A. Hiller, Programming a Computer for Musical Composition, in G. Lekoff (ed.), *Papers from the West Virginia University Conference on Computer Applications in Music,* West Virginia University Library, Morgantown, W. Va., (1967), pp. 63–88.

Example

"Cosahedron"
Second Movement of Algorithm I
for Nine Instruments and One Two-channel Tape
Side 3

This recording closely resembles the latest version three of "Cosahedron." The score was composed by means of a program called MUSI-COMP, written for the IBM 7094 computer. The taped part of the composition was made with the Illiac II computer digital/analog facility by using a special sound-generator program written by Gary Grossman. "Cosahedron" was recorded May 1967 by The University of Illinois Chamber Players and directed by G. Allen O'Conner.

Graphical Language for the Scores of Computer-generated Sounds

M. V. MATHEWS AND L. ROSLER

Bell Telephone Laboratories, Inc.
Murray Hill, New Jersey

ABSTRACT

Conventional scores are an insufficient and inconvenient way of describing sound sequences to computers. A procedure is described for drawing scores as graphical functions of time by using a light pen on a cathode ray tube attached to a small computer. The information is transmitted digitally to a larger computer, which synthesizes the sound and reproduces it immediately with a loudspeaker. Typically, functions for amplitude, frequency, and the duration of a sequence of notes are drawn. An algebra allows combining functions by addition and multiplication. In this way certain compositional processes may be performed by the computer; for example, the time-varying weighted average between two melodic or rhythmic sequences may be synthesized.

The graphical programs provide great flexibility for drawing, copying, erasing, and altering functions. Thus it is easy to develop a sound sequence by a succession of trials. Microfilm and punched-card versions of the score are automatically provided. In addition to being compositional tools, the graphical scores are effective representations of the sound to a listener. In many ways they are easier to follow than conventional scores.

The value of digital computers for generating sound and for simulating speech transmission devices is established [1–4]. Existing programs produce a large variety of sounds with programmed instruments that either simulate real instruments or are wholly artificial. Simple computer languages [5] allow each composer to construct his own unique instruments quickly and easily.

However, specifying the sounds to be produced by these programs can be time consuming. Usually the parameters that specify each sound or note are punched on a computer card. At least five numbers—the instrument to be played, the starting time, duration, frequency, and amplitude—are necessary to specify a single note. Although punching individual note cards is established as a usable composing process, possibilities for improvement exist—possibilities based on better methods of man-computer communication. This article discusses one such approach with a graphic-input computer, the Graphic 1 [6].

The Graphic 1 allows a person to insert pictures and graphs directly into a computer memory by the very act of drawing these objects. Moreover, the power of the computer is available to modify, erase, duplicate, and remember the drawings. A graphical composition language has been invented which allows the score of a piece to be specified as a group of graphs. Thus the full power of the Graphic 1 was applied to the act of composing.

Experiments with graphic scores have already been made by such well-known composers as Varèse, Stockhausen, and Granger. Hence this form of score promised to be both readily developed and powerful. In addition to fulfilling these promises, the scores provided a means of enlisting the computer to assist the composer. Useful algorithms could be written by means of which the computer could generate parts of the music.

The Graphic 1 computer was intended as an aid to engineering designers. It has been applied to a variety of design problems, from electric circuits to mechanical objects.

Designers must specify the details of many interacting parts. Often individual parts are simple, but their interaction is complex. The over-all operation of the device must be kept in mind while concentrating on the details of a particular part.

Viewed in this light, a musical composition is a typical design problem. The over-all structure of the piece must not be forgotten as work is done on the details of a section. The main auditory effects arise from the interactions of many notes that are individually simple.

The Graphic 1 has proved to be a powerful tool for design problems. It is possible to sketch the outlines of objects and fill in the details later. Sometimes the computer can provide the details by means of an algorithm. These design techniques, developed for engineering purposes, may benefit composers as well. In addition, their application to computer music may assist in the development of machine-aided engineering design. Computer sounds have the unique advantage of not only being designable but also being manufacturable on a computer. Thus the finished product is immediately available for evaluation and possible redesign. Such rapid feedback is an ideal laboratory in which to develop design procedures.

The rest of the article presents the details of the graphical scores and algorithms. The section entitled "The Interaction System" reviews the operation of the Graphic 1 computer. "The Graphical-Input Programs" section discusses the special computer language which adapts the

Graphic 1 to the design of compositions. The representation of sound sequences by graphs and the composition algorithms are presented in the section entitled "Specification of Sound Sequences and Music." The appendix provides a complete list of available graphic statements. Finally some acoustic examples are given.

THE INTERACTION SYSTEM

System Organization

The heart of the system is the MUSIC IV program for the IBM 7094 (Figure 1, right) [3, 4, 5]. The input to this program is normally a sequence of symbolic "note" cards, each of which specifies the simulated instrument to be played, the starting time and duration of a note, its amplitude and frequency, and other parameters. The output of the program is a digital magnetic tape that consists of sequential amplitude samples of the generated sound.

In the past it has been necessary to specify the note cards in detail. The graphical language to be described allows these cards to be generated *by a computer program* from simpler data specified in terms of functions, which vary with time in a piece-by-piece linear manner, and their combinations. Although the composer visualizes them as two-dimensional graphs, the actual input to the graphical-score translator (Figure 1, center) consists of card images consisting of alphanumeric data (the coordi-

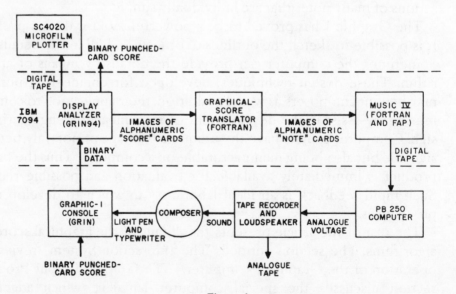

Figure 1

nates of the vertices of the graphs and other numerical descriptors).

The next step in simplification is the introduction of a graphical-input system (Figure 1, left), whose ultimate purpose is to perform the tedious clerical task of reducing the two-dimensional graphs drawn by the composer to the symbolic data cards required by the graphical-score translator. The Graphic 1 console, a computer system with real-time graphical input and display facilities, makes the production and editing of the music functions by the composer a relatively simple and convenient job. It should be stressed, however, that the sound-generating programs in the 7094 computer can alternatively be addressed directly by hand-punched "score" cards, as done in fact before the Graphic 1 console was used.

The output link to the composer, which closes the man-machine interaction loop, consists of the actual sound sequence generated from his graphical input. The digital tape produced by MUSIC IV is rewound and transmitted to another computer (PB250; see Figure 1, right), which converts the amplitude samples into an analog voltage. The voltage is filtered, recorded on magnetic tape, and transmitted to the composer via an amplifier and a loudspeaker. Monaural or stereophonic output may be requested by the composer.

The Graphic 1 Console

The Graphic 1 console is a small computer system equipped with a light pen for graphical input, a typewriter keyboard for alphanumeric input, a card reader for binary input, and a cathode-ray tube for graphical output (Figure 2). Typewriter output is used only for debugging or error messages. The console is "dedicated" to the composer during the course of a composing session and interacts as necessary with the IBM 7094. It would not be economical for the 7094 to be continuously accessible, waiting idly during the composer's thinking time. Instead, the 7094 runs other jobs between the composer's requirements.

The console consists of a DEC PDP-5 computer, a DEC 340 cathode-ray-tube oscilloscope, an Ampex RVQ buffer memory, and appropriate hardware interfaces (Figure 3). The information stored in the Ampex consists primarily of instructions that may be decoded to create a display on the face of the cathode-ray tube. In addition, the Ampex can store nondisplay data; for example, encoded descriptions of the various displayable elements.

The name of the light pen is deceptive. It is not a light-generating device but rather a light-sensing device. In fact, it is a shutter-equipped, flexible, fiber-optics tube connected to a photocell in the computer cabinet. The photocell signals the computer when it detects light, and the

Figure 2

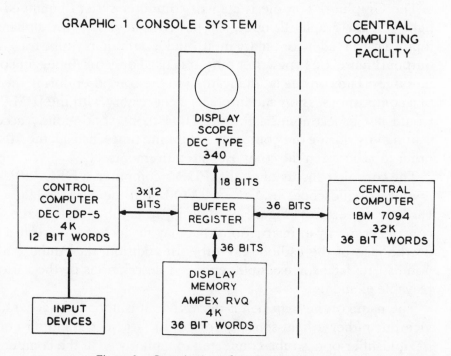

Figure 3. Organization of the Graphic 1 console.

coordinates of the cathode-ray-tube beam at that time can be recorded by the program.

The GRIN (GRaphical INput) language [7] for the Graphic 1 console includes two commands by means of which data can be supplied by the light pen to answer the questions "where" and "which."

To answer the question "where," a tracking cross is displayed 60 times a second. The program attempts to keep the cross centered in the field of view of the light pen. The cross thus allows positional information to be conveyed to the program, even where nothing is being displayed.

To answer the question "which," the operator points the light pen at an entity displayed on the screen, for example, a word of text. The program determines the entity being pointed at and causes it to be intensi-fied, thus providing visual feedback to confirm the operator's choice. The program can then take alternate actions, depending on the entity selected by the operator.

The oscilloscope thus serves three functions. It presents a selective display of the contents of the Ampex memory, a drawing surface on which to use the light pen, and a control surface on which various control segments may be displayed, with mnemonic shapes or labels supplied by the programmer. These so-called "light buttons," when pointed to by the light pen, cause entry to specific subprograms. Because the light buttons are tailored to fit the problem to be solved, they constitute a problem-oriented language, the only computer-control language that the composer need learn. This use of the display surface for control has many advantages: the attention of the operator need not be diverted from the display; the display is flexible, and thus only those control functions that are meaningful at the moment are presented to the operator; and appro-priate messages can be displayed to the operator to direct him to supply the data required by the various subprograms. Thus the program itself instructs the composer in its own use.

THE GRAPHICAL-INPUT PROGRAMS

The Graphic 1 GRIN Program

The GRIN program used for the generation of graphical scores di-vides the display surface into two areas: a region for light buttons and messages to the composer and a grid on which the music functions are drawn.

Figure 4 is a view reproduced from microfilm of the blank display sur-face seen by the composer. A microfilm of the display is automatically

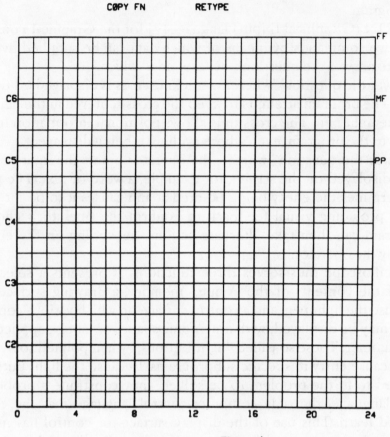

Figure 4

provided each time the composer interacts with the IBM 7094. These microfilms provide an essential record of the score. The examples given in this article are all prepared from these microfilms.

The abscissa of the grid is the duration either in beats or in arbitrary units proportional to time. Standard scales for pitch or loudness are provided for the ordinate; different scales can be specified by the composer. The grid is included in all the microfilm output generated by the 7094. For clarity of presentation in this article the minor grid structure has been suppressed in later figures by a temporary modification in the program.

The light buttons and their operations are listed in the appendix, but here we describe the typical way in which the buttons are used. Information constituting the score consists of graphic functions drawn on the grid with line segments and followed by a line of text consisting of a three-letter label and two or more numerical parameters.

The FUNCTN button is used to draw most of the functions. Because of the self-explanatory nature of the light buttons and the liberal use of messages to the user, which are displayed on the scope, the process can be learned with little effort.

When the light pen is pointed at the FUNCTN button, a tracking cross appears, and the light buttons are replaced by a message that tells the composer to move the cross to the starting point of the function, which he indicates by pushing a button when the cross is positioned to his satisfaction. A temporary vector then appears, which joins the tracking cross to the starting point with a "rubber-band" effect. A new message tells the composer to fix the successive vertices of the function permanently by pushing the button each time the cross is properly positioned. The composer completes the function by pushing a second button and is asked to type a line of descriptive text. The program then asks the composer to indicate (via the light pen on a new set of light buttons) whether he has made any typing errors. If he has, he must retype the descriptor; if he has not, the main light buttons are displayed again and a new command may be initiated.

Other light buttons permit copying, deleting, and moving functions. One asks for an interaction with the IBM 7094 to play a completed score. Another loads punched cards containing a previously drawn score in machine-readable form into the Graphic 1 memory.

The graphical score may be written onto any one of 12 frames. A particular frame is displayed on the scope by a light button, and a second frame may then be overlayed on the scope face. In this way frames can be compared and functions copied from one frame into another.

The 7094 GRIN94 Program

The 7094 program that interacts with the Graphic 1 console is written in GRIN94 [8], a development of GRIN. The input consists solely of the contents of the Graphic 1 memory—that is, the display the composer has generated. Each frame is scanned in sequence for music functions. When a music function is found, the coordinates of its vertices are written sequentially onto a magnetic-disk file, followed by the typed descriptor of the function. This file is then presented as input to the graphical-score translator program.

In addition, a hard-copy permanent score is created by reproducing on microfilm each of the 12 frames that contain at least one music function, together with its identifying frame letter and the date and time of the interaction. A permanent copy of the graphical score in compact computer-readable form is also generated. This is a binary deck which later may be reloaded into the Graphic 1 or the 7094 and edited and reprocessed by the composer. This permits the composer to resume an interrupted session from the point of the most recent interaction without having to regenerate all his input manually.

Specification of Sound Sequences and Music

How can these graphical facilities be used for the description of sound sequences? We first describe the simple representation of a sequence of sounds by graphic functions. Then we describe a number of special procedures for composing with these functions. These composing algorithms are some of the most interesting results of the graphical language.

Simple Specification of Sound Sequences

The essential features of the method for specifying sound sequences can best be brought out by presenting a few examples. A more detailed specification of the graphic language is given in the appendix. One form of the score for the first four measures (eight beats) of the march "The British Grenadiers" is shown in Figure 5. The four functions required specify amplitude, frequency, note durations, and any glissando (continuously changing frequency) that may be used. The conventional music score for this fragment is shown in Figure 6 for comparison. On the graphic score two abscissa units equals one beat.

The upper function describes amplitude and is labeled AMP. The standard scale for amplitude is indicated along the upper right margin of the graph, going from *PP* to *FF*. This particular function puts an accent on the first half-beat of each measure and plays the rest of the measure at a uniform amplitude. The "1" following the label AMP is a count indicating that one additional number is to follow. The "2" indicates that the function is two beats long. All functions are periodic and are repeated as many times as appropriate. A nonperiodic function may be constructed by using only one period of a periodic function. The positioning of the drawing from beats 12 to 16 on the abscissa has no significance; the periodic function will start at the beginning each time it is used.

The frequency function is shown immediately below the amplitude function and is labeled FRE. The normal frequency scale is shown on the left-hand side of the graph, C4 being the fourth C on the piano (middle C), C5 being an octave above, C3, an octave below, and so forth. The numerical value of the frequency ordinate is equal to the logarithm to the base 2 of the ratio of the frequency to middle C (262 cps). Thus C4 is zero, C5 is +1, and so on. For this particular composition a more ex-

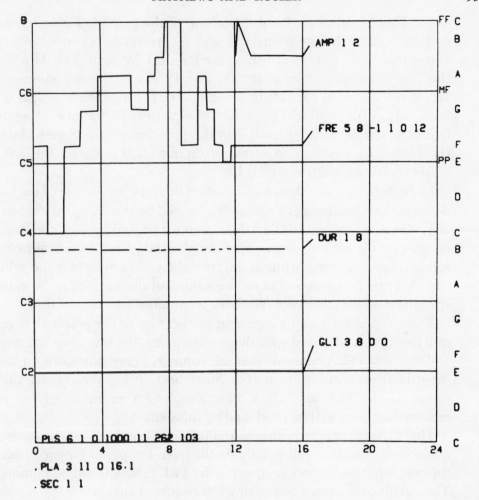

Figure 5

Figure 6

panded diatonic scale, which has been labeled along the right-hand side
C, D, E, . . ., is appropriate. These labels, written with the COMMENT
light button, are for the composer's benefit only. The program ignores
them. Five numbers are written after the count following FRE. The "8"
indicates that the duration of the function is eight beats. The correspondence between beats and time is made by a standard metronome marking, not shown. This piece is played at a rate of 110 beats per minute.

The -1 and 1 label the bottom and top of the graph, -1 corresponding to C an octave below middle C and 1 corresponding to C an octave above middle C, thus establishing the scale on the right. The 0 following the 1 is not used in this example. The 12 is an arbitrary number that labels the function for future reference in the algebra and also is not used here. In general it is necessary to type only the numbers that differ from the standard scales built into the program. Thus, if we had drawn the frequency function in terms of the standard scale on the left, we could simply have written FRE 1 8.

Note durations are shown as a dashed line, the beginning of each dash denoting the beginning of the note, the end of the dash, the end of the note. Glissando is not used in this composition and has been eliminated by making the frequency range of the glissando from 0 to 0. When glissando is used, the logarithm of the frequency of each note is the value of the FRE function sampled at the beginning of the note, plus the value of the glissando function generated as a continuous function of time.

Three typed statements appear at the bottom of the graph. (There are null functions associated with these statements; the functions are unused and invisible.) PLA requests that the computer play this score on instrument 11 from beat 0 to beat 16.1. Since beat 16.1 is about twice the duration of the FRE and DUR functions, two repetitions of the four-measure sections will be produced by this demand.

The PLS statement requests a subroutine to quantize the note frequencies so that they fall exactly on the even-tempered F-major scale. In this way any small errors in drawing the FRE function will be eliminated. The details of the pitch quantizing are discussed later.

The line labeled SEC terminates this section of the composition. The scores are all divided into sections, each of which starts at beat 0 and lasts until the last note called on by any play instruction is completed.

An alternative, more compact and intuitive specification of the same score, is shown on Figure 7. The principal difference is that the frequency and durational functions have been combined into a single function labeled DUF. Frequencies are read as the ordinate to the DUF function and durations as the abscissa. The glissando function has not been drawn out, but it is specified by an algebraic statement FGL that says that the glissando shall be calculated as the sum of function 10, plus function 10. Function 10, one of two standard functions built into the program, is identically zero, and so glissando is eliminated. The details of the algebra, of which FGL is an example, is elaborated in the next section. The other statements are similar to those presented in Figure 5. The PLA plays two cycles of the composition, starting at beat 1; hence there will be a one-beat rest at the beginning of the section that will separate it from the end

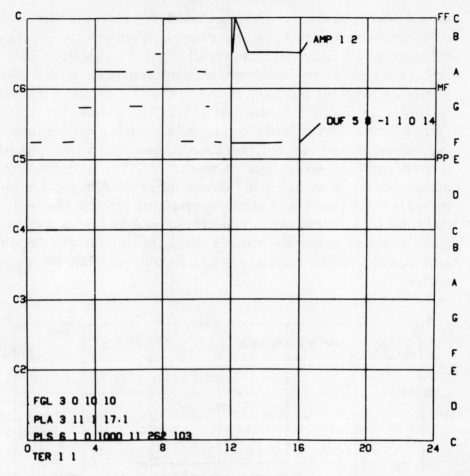

Figure 7

of the preceding section. The entire composition is ended by the TER statement.

Algebra for Combining Functions

The direct graphical specification of sound sequences described above is a simpler, faster, and surer method of putting this information into a computer than punching the equivalent numbers on computer cards. However, many additional features have been added to the graphical language. One is an algebra for combining graphical functions, which is especially useful for computer-aided composition. By means of this language the computer can do many things. For example, it can average between two melodic or rhythmic lines or gradually convert one rhythmic or melodic pattern into another. These averaging processes have produced pleasing results, particularly in view of the simplicity of the algorithm involved. As another example, it can combine functions of different periods to produce an over-all function with a much longer period. Such a process frequently produces interesting sequences.

An example of the averaging process is shown in Figures 8 through 11. In this example "The British Grenadiers" is gradually converted to "When Johnny Comes Marching Home" and back, a nauseating musical experience but one not without interest, particularly in the rhythmic conversions. "The Grenadiers" is written in 2/4 time in the key of F major. "Johnny" is written in 6/8 time in the key of E minor. The change from 2/4 to 6/8 time can be clearly appreciated, yet would be quite difficult for a human musician to play. The modulation from the key of F major to E minor, which involves a change of two notes in the scale, is jarring, and a smaller transition would undoubtedly have been a better choice.

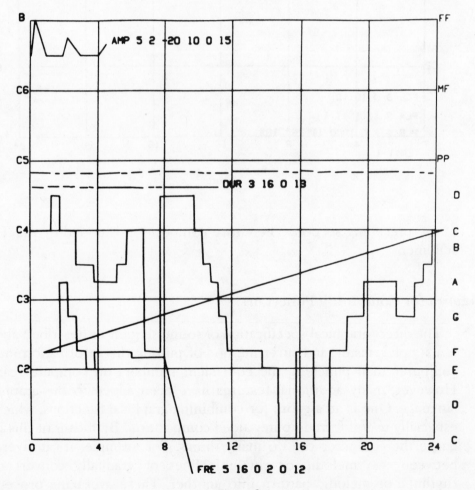

Figure 8

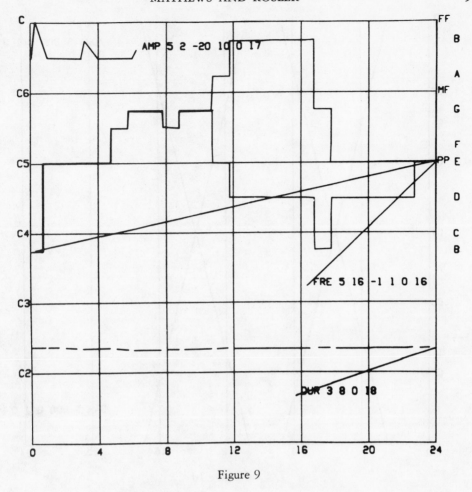

Figure 9

Sixteen beats of "The British Grenadiers" are drawn in Figure 8. Because it is inconvenient and inaccurate to draw this number of beats across a single page, the frequency and duration functions have, in effect, been continued onto two pages. The drawing surface can be considered as a cylinder, with its right-hand side joined to the left-hand side. Functions can be continued by moving the pen back to the left-hand side and continuing to draw, as is shown clearly for the frequency function. The amplitude function produces both a primary and a secondary accent in each measure. Two units along the abscissa correspond to one beat. Thus the measures are indicated by the major abscissa divisions. The frequency function has been labeled 12, the duration function, 13, and the amplitude function, 15, for future reference in the algebra.

Figure 9 shows the corresponding score for "Johnny." In this score it is convenient to make one beat of the 6/8 time equivalent to one abscissa unit. The entire eight-measure (48-beat) section takes 48 abscissa units to draw. The duration of this eight-measure section is 16 beats of the

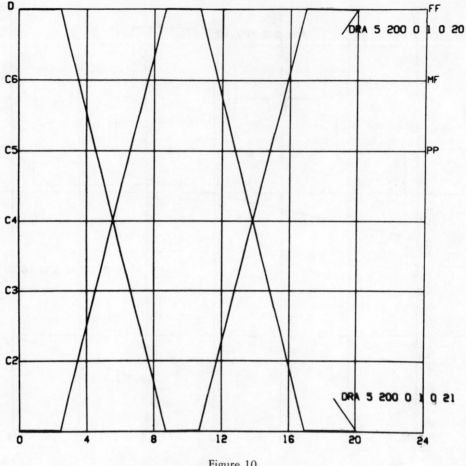

Figure 10

composition; thus one measure of "Johnny" will correspond exactly to one measure of "The Grenadiers." The duration line in "Johnny" happens to repeat exactly after four measures, and only four measures need be drawn. Again the amplitude function shows a primary and secondary accent. The amplitude, frequency, and duration functions are labeled 17, 16, and 18, respectively.

The two averaging functions are shown in Figure 10. In the algebra the frequency and duration function of "The Grenadiers" will be multiplied by function 20. Function 20 has a duration of 200 beats, compared with the 16-beat duration for one cycle of either melody. Its value is unity for the first 24 beats; it then decreases linearly to zero. It remains zero for 24 beats, and increases back to unity for the last 30 beats. The complementary function 21 starts at zero, builds up to unity in the middle, and decreases to zero at the end. The melodic line of the resulting composition will be formed as the sum of the melodic line of "The Grenadiers" multiplied by function 20, plus the melodic line of "Johnny" multiplied by function 21. Thus the melody will start with "The British Grenadiers," gradually be converted to "Johnny" and be reconverted to "The Grenadiers."

One step in addition to averaging is required. The weighted average between simultaneous notes in "The Grenadiers" and in "Johnny" would, in general, be a frequency not necessarily belonging to the scale of either "The Grenadiers" or "Johnny." Thus the average is quantized against a scale that contains all the notes in either the scale of F major or E minor; that is C, D, E, F#, G, A, B♭, and B.

The rhythmic functions are averaged in a manner similar to the frequency functions. The particular way in which the rhythm pattern is represented in the computer to allow such averaging is discussed in detail in the next section. For the moment we simply state that the averaging process works like any other averaging.

The actual statements to the computer to perform the algebra are

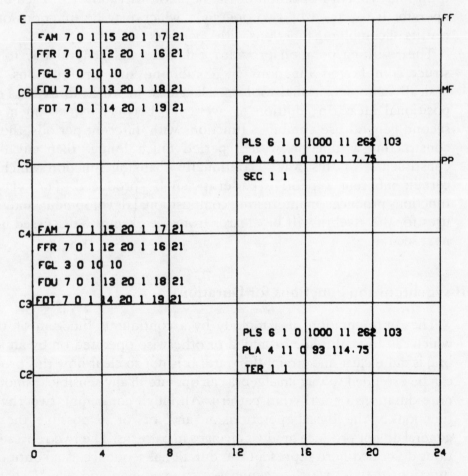

Figure 11

shown on Figure 11. For convenience in programming these statements have been written in numerical parentheses-free notation, which uses binary operators placed as prefixes [9]. This notation is admittedly difficult to write and read, and in subsequent versions of the program it can easily be replaced by something more attractive.

Two operators are currently included: addition (represented by 0) and multiplication (represented by 1). Space is reserved in the program for other operators represented by the digits 2 through 9. Functions are represented by function numbers 10 through 89. Function 10 is a built-in function equal to zero; function 11 is a built-in function equal to unity.

As an example, the top line on Figure 11 instructs the computer to form an amplitude function, which in more conventional notation would be written

$$\text{amplitude function} = [F_{15}(t) \times F_{20}(t)] + [F_{17}(t) \times F_{21}(t)]$$

The functions 15, 17, 20, and 21 have already been defined in Figures 8 through 10. An inspection of the notation will show that each binary operator is followed by two operands, which may be functions or the results of combining functions with operators.

The resulting notation provides a flexible and general way to construct complicated functions by combining simpler functions. It is basically a compositional tool or a language in which to express compositional ideas. In addition to averaging between two sequences, a second general use combines functions with different periods, thereby constructing a function with a period much longer than any of its constituents. In this way a continually changing function which has certain inherent repetitive patterns can be produced. This class of functions produces an interesting compositional development, and these uses for the algebra will be clearer from the examples discussed in the next section.

Self-synchronizing Functions for Durations

The representation of a melody by a continuous function of time, which can be multiplied or added or otherwise operated on by an algebra, is quite clear and straightforward. It is not so clear how this process can be extended so that an algebra can operate in any sensible fashion on note durations or a rhythm pattern. Although combining two rhythm functions by the logical operations of "and" or "or" is possible, these in general do not produce gradual changes in patterns. The two representations described here represent the durational sequence as a continuous function of time, which is amenable to averaging and which changes rhythm patterns in a manner that sounds reasonable. In other words, one pattern is converted to another pattern by lengthening or shortening the notes that might be expected to change and by adding or subtracting notes at appropriate times if the two patterns have different numbers of notes.

Although a durational pattern is drawn as a sequence of dashes on the score, it is represented in the computer by a continuous function of time of the type in Figure 12. Here a five-beat pattern is shown with the conventional score for this pattern. The computer generates the rhythm pattern by operating on the stored function $f_1(t)$ with a standard algorithm. At the start of the pattern the algorithm reads the initial value of f_1, $f_1(0)$ and obtains the duration of the first note, 1.5 beats. It then generates a note 1.5 beats long and reads the value of f_1 at the beginning of the second note, $f_1(1.5)$. The value of the function is 0.5, the duration of the second note. The computer generates this note and then reads function $f_1(2)$ to obtain the duration of the third note, and so on. The function repeats at the end of five beats. Between the points marking the durations of the notes the function is made up of line segments with a slope of -1 and discontinuities joining successive line segments. These discontinuities are arbitrarily located halfway between the starting points of successive notes. This rather peculiar shape of function was chosen because it makes the rhythm function invariant both to computational errors and to small changes introduced by the algebra. We refer to this form as a self-synchronizing function; for example, if the function is initially sampled not at zero but at some small time after zero, the slope of the function will produce a note just enough shorter than 1.5 beats so that the second

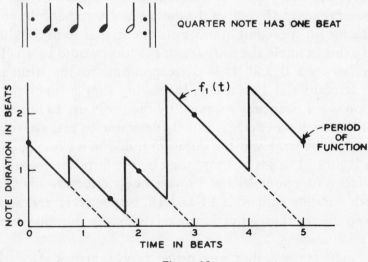

QUARTER NOTE HAS ONE BEAT

Figure 12

note will occur at its normal starting time of 1.5 beats. In general, if a self-synchronizing function is entered at some point other than the starting time of one of the preplanned notes, one odd-length note will be produced and the subsequent sequence will be as planned. A number of experiments have shown that this self-synchronization property is useful in maintaining the character of a rhythmic sequence in the face of the algorithmic changes made in a computer development.

The self-synchronizing function has a second pleasant property. If $f_1(t)$ and $f_2(t)$ are the self-synchronizing functions that represent two different rhythmic sequences, any average $f_3(t)$ between these two,

$$f_3(t) = a f_1(t) + (1 - a) f_2(t), \qquad 0 \le a \le 1,$$

is also a self-synchronizing function. This property occurs because $f_1(t)$ and $f_2(t)$ are formed entirely of line segments with a slope of -1 and discontinuities; hence $f_3(t)$ must also be of the same nature. It is obvious that when a is 1, $f_3(t)$ equals $f_1(t)$, and when a is zero $f_3(t)$ equals $f_2(t)$. Experimentally it has turned out that the development between rhythm pattern 1 and rhythm pattern 2 as a changes is both interesting and orderly for many rhythm patterns. This process allows the algebraic averaging described in the preceding section to be applied to rhythm patterns. We find it a most useful compositional tool.

We have omitted one detail in the description of the rhythm function —the duty-factor function. The duration function specifies the time between the beginning of one note and the beginning of the next. The duty-factor function specifies the portion of time during which the note is actually playing, thus controlling the degree of legato or staccato in the style. In drawing the duration function, as, for example, function 13 in Figure 8, the duty factor is inherent in the length of the dashes. The computer reads the length of the dashes and automatically constructs the duty-factor function and numbers it one higher than the duration function. In this example the duty-factor function would be 14. The function varies between 0 and 1, 0 corresponding to the ultimate and vanishing staccato and 1 to a slur. In playing simple tunes the duty-factor function is automatically supplied by the program. In more complicated algebraic developments it is usually desirable to average the duty-factor function in the same way the duration function is averaged. In the example in Figure 11 this is accomplished by the fifth statement from the top. Duty-factor functions 14 and 19 have been automatically constructed to go with duration functions 13 and 18, respectively; the algebraic statement combines these functions exactly as the duration functions have been combined.

We may ask whether any other representations for rhythmic sequences have the same properties as the self-synchronizing functions we have just described? An alternative computer rhythm function is shown in Figure 13. Here the start of a note is represented by the positive-going zero crossing of a function and the termination of the note by the subsequent negative-going zero crossing. As shown, the function is made up of straight-line segments, but any function with a succession of zero crossings could be used. Two of the zero-crossing representations may be averaged in exactly the same way as the self-synchronizing functions are averaged. We have not tried this process, but it appears that the average would have desirable psychoacoustic properties. The zero-crossing representation is even more general than the self-synchronizing function in that almost any algebraic operation on it will produce a legitimate rhythmic sequence, whereas allowable operations on self-synchronizing functions are basically limited to weighted averaging. However, the zero-crossing representation would necessitate a searching process to find the zero crossings of the function when generating the rhythmic sequence; this process may be difficult and time consuming on the computer.

Whichever process is used to represent durations, the over-all result is the addition of a powerful development tool to the composer's arsenal of algorithms. The rhythmic averaging seems to be even more interesting than the frequency averaging and to make more psychoacoustic sense.

Metronome Markings

Metronome markings, which give the relation between beats in the score and seconds of time in the sound, have not been shown in any of the figures. They are treated exactly as described in the MUSIC IV Manual [5]. A numerical function made up of straight-line segments specifies the tempo in terms of the standard metronome mark beats

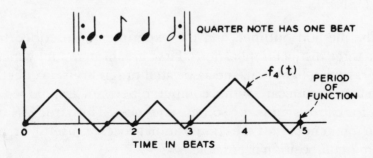

Figure 13

per minute. The tempo may change continuously with time to introduce accelerandos or retards; for example, the statement

NUM 9 801 0 0 0 60 100 150 200 125

would specify at beat 0 a tempo of 60 beats/min, which is increased linearly at beat 100 to a tempo of 150 beats/sec. This then decreases at beat 200 to a tempo of 125 beats/sec. In this case the tempo function consists of two straight-line segments, one specifying an accelerando, the other a retard. As many segments as desired may be specified, thus approximating any given tempo as closely as desired.

Pitch Quantizing

The PLS statement used in conjunction with frequency averaging requests a subroutine in the music program to quantize the frequencies of notes from the graphic functions. The pitch quantizing has already been described [10]. The purpose of the subroutine is to change the frequency of a note to equal the closest scale step of a prespecified scale. In this way any small inaccuracies introduced in drawing the frequency function can be eliminated.

In the PLS statement in Figure 5 the particular scale is described by numbers 262 (which gives the frequency of the fundamental of the scale in cycles per second) and 103 (which specifies the intervals in the scale). In this case function 103 would contain the logarithmic intervals 0, 0.167, 0.333, 0.417, 0.583, 0.75, and 0.8333, corresponding, respectively, to C, D, E, F, G, A, and B$\flat$.

It is also possible to use the pitch-quantizing program to adjust the pitch of a note in a voice so that it will form one of a set of allowable intervals with the note in a second voice playing at the same time. In this way it is possible to control the harmonic structure of the composition.

CONCLUSIONS

The method outlined and the experiments described in this article have three distinct implications. First, graphical input by means of a cathode-ray tube, light pen, and associated programs is an effective way for a man to communicate with a computer. Second, graphic scores are excellent for expressing many sound sequences. Third, the use of algorithms as an inherent part of the composition process is useful, or, in short, algorithmic composition is possible.

1. By means of the graphical-input computer the composer is freed

from the clerical drudgery of transcribing his scores into computer-readable form. Errors in the scores are immediately apparent and can be easily corrected by using the editing facilities of the graphical terminal. Hard-copy and machine-readable forms of the scores are produced. Finally, the use of a more-or-less real-time interaction system allows the composer to *hear* the sound sequence he has specified almost immediately and make appropriate changes. Thus effective use is made of the best capabilities of both participants in the creative process—the machine supplying computational power, the human supplying judgment and direction as needed.

2. Graphic scores describe a sequence of sounds by three basic graphical functions; these functions, in turn, specify the pitch, the note durations, and the loudness. The first two functions may be combined in a single line if desired.

The scores for electronic pieces serve two basic functions. They help the composer to organize and remember his ideas; they help the listener to follow and learn the composition. Our experience leads us to believe graphic scores are substantially better than conventional scores for both purposes. It is certainly easier to sketch and review ideas graphically. Details can be filled in or left out, and the general development of passages can easily be seen. Melodies may be followed in general or in detail. In addition, we suspect that the graphic scores will be easier to learn to read than conventional scores. The expression of pitch as a position in the ordinate direction (free of the restrictions imposed by the music clef) and duration as a length in the abscissa direction (rather than an encoded "note" symbol) has direct intuitive validity.

It seems doubtful that graphic scores will replace conventional parts for instrumentalists playing a piece. However, the graphic language poses a generality for describing computer and electronic music that is completely beyond the capabilities of conventional scores. We expect that much of the music of the future will be scored graphically.

3. The basic tools for algorithmic composition which have proved effective are the periodic function, the algebra for combining these functions, the self-synchronizing function to represent durations, and the pitch-quantizing subroutine. These devices are used principally to average between melodic and rhythmic patterns and to generate multiperiodic sequences in which functions with different periods are combined. A particularly effective combination consists of a melodic and a rhythmic line of slightly different periods.

By means of these algorithms many of the details of generating individual notes need not be completely written out. The composer can control the loudness, tempo, and number of voices by simple global functions that directly express his musical intentions. He can, with only slightly more work, control the degree of syncopation or synchronization between voices as well as the harmony and scale.

Is the computer composing? The question is best unasked, but it cannot be completely ignored. An answer is difficult to provide. The algorithms are deterministic, simple, and understandable. No complicated or hard-to-understand computations are involved; no "learning" programs are used; no random processes occur; the machine functions in a perfectly mechanical and straightforward manner. However, the result is sequences of sound that are unplanned in fine detail by the composer, even though the over-all structure of the section is completely and precisely specified. Thus the composer is often surprised, and pleasantly surprised, at the details of the realization of his ideas. To this extent only is the computer composing. We call the process algorithmic composition, but we immediately re-emphasize that the algorithms are transparently simple.

We believe algorithmic composition is the beginning of a revolution in the musical use of computers. The potentialities for composers of recorded pieces should already be clear. Additional possibilities will shortly be put forward when computers become fast and cheap enough for improvisation. The examples in this paper made considerable use of averaging functions for gradually modifying rhythmic and melodic sequences. These functions changed slowly with time in a predetermined manner. They, rather than the individual notes, can be under the direct control of the musician as he improvises. He can linger near the averages that interest him and pass quickly through uninteresting combinations.

Finally, the compositional algorithms can be used to supplement technical knowledge, thus allowing music to be composed by people without formal training. If the day comes when each house has its own computer terminal, these techniques may make music as a means of self-expression accessible to everyone.

REFERENCES

[1] E. E. David, Jr., M. V. Mathews, and H. S. McDonald, A High-Speed Data Translator for Computer Simulation of Speech and Television Devices, *Proc. Western Joint Computer Conf.* (1959).

[2] M. V. Mathews, An Acoustic Compiler for Music and Psychological Stimuli, *Bell System Tech. J.,* **40,** 677–694 (1961).

[3] M. V. Mathews, The Digital Computer as a Musical Instrument, *Science,* **142,** 553–557 (1963).

[4] J. R. Pierce, M. V. Mathews, and J. C. Risset, Further Experiments on the Use of the Computer in Connection with Music, *Gravesaner Blatter,* **27/28,** 92–97 (1965).

[5] M. V. Mathews and Joan A. Miller, *MUSIC IV Programmer's Manual,* Bell Telephone Laboratories, Murray Hill, N.J. (unpublished).

[6] W. H. Ninke, GRAPHIC 1—A Remote Graphical Display Console System, *Proc. Fall Joint Computer Conf.,* **27,** 839 (1965).

[7] C. Christensen, *GRIN (GRaphical INput) Language for the Graphic-1 Console,* Bell Telephone Laboratories, Murray Hill, N.J. (unpublished).

[8] L. Rosler, *The Graphic-1 7094 Graphical Interaction System and the GRIN94 Language,* Bell Telephone Laboratories, Murray Hill, N.J. (unpublished).

[9] J. Lukasiewicz, *Elements of Mathematical Logic,* Warsaw (1929).

[10] M. V. Mathews and Joan E. Miller, Pitch Quantizing for Computer Music, *J. Acoust. Soc. Am.,* **38,** 913(A) (1965).

Examples

The effectiveness of the graphical scores and composing algorithms may best be judged from actual recordings of the sounds so generated. Program notes that describe the examples are presented here.

1. *Rhythm Developments*
Side 5, Band 1

Several initial experiments that converted one rhythm pattern to another by a time-varying weighted average were carried out, as is discussed under "Specification of Sound Sequences and Music." Four short examples are produced on Side 5, Band 1, and their scores given in Figure 14. In each case rhythm pattern *A* is converted to rhythm pattern *B* by multiplying pattern *A* with a linearly decreasing weighting function and adding it to pattern *B* with a linearly increasing weighting function.

Transition No. 1. This change occurs very slowly, so that the duration variations of individual notes and the introduction of new notes into pattern *A* can be clearly heard.

Transition No. 2. This is a considerably more interesting and much more rapid change than Transition No. 1. Unexpectedly, our perception tends to synchronize on the third note of pattern *A* as the starting point of the pattern rather than the initial note.

Transition No. 3. Pattern *A* of this transition is similar to pattern *A* of Transition No. 2, except that a note has been added to make the first note of the pattern perceived as drawn. Pattern *B* is similar to pattern *A*; hence the transition between the two patterns occurs very quickly. The length and character of the transition strongly depends on the patterns themselves.

Transition No. 4. Two simple patterns consisting of three notes per measure and four notes per measure are involved; the resulting transition displays several unexpected subtleties. We can first perceive changes in durations of the initial three notes; then a fourth note is

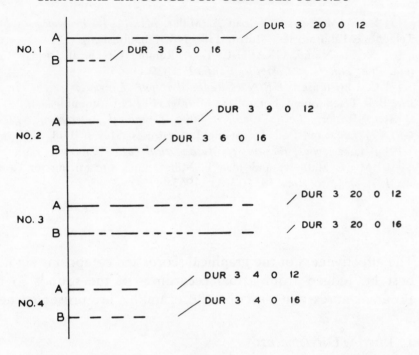

Figure 14

added. The durations of the four notes are changed until finally a regular four-note group is achieved. Perceptually we tend to anticipate the approach of regularity in the four-note group and hear the grouping as regular before equal time divisions have been achieved. A half-speed and a normal-speed version of the transition are on the tape.

2. *The British Grenadiers–Johnny Comes Marching Home*

   Side 5, Band 2

The score for this development is presented in Figures 8–11 and discussed on pp. 96-100. We add only a few comments here. "The Grenadiers" is in 2/4 time and divides the measure strongly into four parts and "Johnny" is in 6/8 time and divides the measure strongly into six parts, an interesting rhythmic transition occurs between these prominent and contradictory patterns. The result can easily be appreciated after hearing the example. A good percussion player said that it would be very difficult to play because of the problem of desynchronizing oneself from the 2/4 time and changing to the 6/8.

3. *The International Lullaby*

   Side 6, Band 1

This example consists of the computer development of a Japanese lullaby into the well-known Schubert "Cradle Song." The Japanese melody is written in a pentatonic scale with the notes C, D, E♭, G, and A♭. The "Cradle Song" is written in the key of C. The portions of both melodies last 16 beats and both have essentially two beats per measure, although the accents in the Japanese melody frequently occur on the second quarter of the first beat.

The computer is used to average the rhythm and the melodic lines between these two melodies. The total development takes 112 beats (seven repetitions). The weighting function used to average melody and rhythm is stairstep in shape, as shown in Figure 15. One 16-beat cycle is played on each step.

The average pitch is quantized into a scale containing all the frequencies in the Schubert and Japanese scales; that is C, D, E♭, E, F, G, A♭, A, and B. Three versions of the development are presented. The first is a single voice going from the Japanese lullaby to Schubert. The second is a single voice going from Schubert to the Japanese lullaby by the inverse path. The third contains two voices, a pitched voice and a band-pass noise. The pitched voice goes from the Japanese to Schubert as in the first version. The band-pass noise is introduced in the middle five sections. The center frequency of the noise exactly repeats the Japanese melody five times. The durations of the notes, however, are changed from the Japanese to Schubert, so that the notes are in synchrony with the pitched voice. In the stereophonic version the pitched and noise voices exchange speakers during the course of the piece.

The Japanese-to-Schubert computer development is pleasing in both its rhythmic and frequency lines. To listeners with a background of Western music, in the first hearing, the Schubert lullaby was recognizable in the Japanese-to-Schubert transition only in its pure form. In sub-

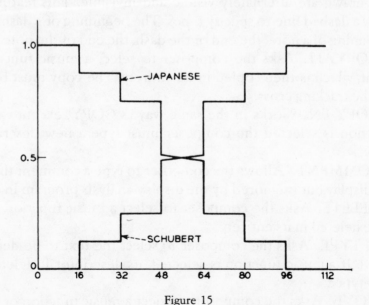

Figure 15

sequent hearings the development into the Schubert lullaby could be clearly perceived in the fifth and sixth steps of the averaging function. Conversely, after the first hearing it was not possible to detect the deviations from the original Japanese melody in the second step. However, in subsequent hearings the deviations could be noted clearly. On the other hand, in the transition from Schubert to Japanese the first changed note in the second step stands out prominently. A Japanese listener would doubtless have quite different and perhaps inverse reactions.

APPENDIX LIGHT BUTTONS AND OPERATION CODES FOR GRAPHIC SCORES

Information is generated on the Graphic 1 by a set of 13 light buttons, a light pen, and a typewriter keyboard. We describe the operation of the light buttons.

FUNCTN. A tracking cross appears; the cross is moved with the light pen to the starting point of the function. Button No. 1 is pressed to mark this point; the cross is moved to the next point on the function. Button No. 1 is pressed again to mark this point, and so on. Up to 100 points can be designated in this manner. Straight-line segments, visible on the scope, connect the points. The function is completed by pushing a second button. A line of text must then be typed; it is terminated by typing a special escape character. The line can then be accepted or deleted and retyped in case of error.

NOTES. Works in the same way as FUNCTN, except that the vectors drawn are alternately visible and invisible. This feature is used to draw a dashed line to specify times. The beginning of a dash specifies the beginning of a note; the end of the dash, the end of the note.

COPYALL. Asks the composer to select a music function or comment, which is then copied in its entirety. The copy must be positioned via the tracking cross.

COPY FN. Works in the same way as COPY, except that if a music function is selected the composer must type a new descriptor for the copy.

COMMENT. Allows the composer to type a comment that appears in the display but is ignored by the display-analysis program in the 7094.

DELETE. Asks the composer to select a music function or comment to be deleted in its entirety.

RETYPE. Asks the composer to select the text to be deleted and retyped. If a music function is selected, its descriptor is deleted and must be retyped.

MOVE. Asks the composer to select a music function or comment to be moved via the tracking cross. A music function and its descriptor move together.

7094. Sets a signal for the 7094, which services the request on completing the job currently being processed. The waiting time varies from a few seconds to (typically) a few minutes.

LOAD. Allows the composer to load from the card reader a binary deck containing a score previously punched by the 7094 display-analysis program.

CLEAR. Clears the frame currently being displayed.

FRAME. Asks the composer to select the frame to be displayed and into which the succeeding new data are to be placed. A list of 12 frames lettered A to L is presented.

OVERLAY. Asks the composer to select the frame to be overlayed. The overlayed frame is displayed less brightly than the frame into which new data are being placed. Entities in the overlayed frame may be moved, copied, or deleted.

The form of information conveyed to the music program in the 7094 consists of a graphic function followed by a typed operation code and two or more numbers. A listing and description of these codes is given next.

The operation code is a three-letter mnemonic that specifies the purpose of the function just drawn. The first number is a word count that gives the number of numbers to follow. The rest of the numbers have various meanings for various operations. Numbers can be separated either by blank spaces or by a comma. The numbers may or may not contain decimal points.

In general only two numbers need be written after an operation code. Subsequent numbers, if not written, are given standard values by the program in some cases. They are called default values and are indicated in the description below.

Functions can be explicitly numbered from 12 through 49. If this is not done, the program will automatically number successive functions sequentially from 50 through 89.

Functions 10 and 11 are predefined as zero and unity, respectively, for all values of abscissa. In the following list

W is the word count.
P is the period of function in beats.
B is the value given the bottom line of grid.
T is the value given the top line of grid.
F is the function number.

Default values when used are given in parentheses.

AMP — Draw amplitude function
AMP   W   P   B(-20)   T(10)   O   F

GLI — Draw glissando function
GLI   W   P   B(-3)   T(3)   O   F

FRE — Draw frequency function
FRE   W   P   B(-3)   T(3)   O   F

DUR — Draw duration function
DUR   W   P   O   F

Note that the program automatically constructs a duty-factor function to go with a DUR function and numbers it $F + 1$.

FAM — Compute amplitude function.
FAM   W N_1 N_2 $N_3 \ldots N_w$

$N_i = O$ stands for addition

$N_i = 1$ stands for multiplication

$10 \leq N_i < 89$ refers to functions by number

Example: The statement

FAM   9   1   0   1   12   13   0   14   15   16

is equivalent to

$$(((F_{12} \times F_{13}) + (F_{14} + F_{15})) \times F_{16})$$

FGL — Compute glissando function   Notation

FFR — Compute frequency function   is the

FDU — Compute duration function   same as

FDT — Compute duty-factor function   FAM

Note that the program *does not* automatically compute an FDT function, and a function corresponding to the FDU must be written out. See the examples in Figure 11.

DRA — Draw a general function that can be used in an algebraic statement

DRA   W   P   B   T   O   F

PLA — Play a sequence of notes

Form 1. PLA   3   V   B   E

    V is the instrument number;

    B is the beginning beat of sound;

    E is the ending beat of sound;

    All functions involved in the generation start at zero (abscissa) at beat B.

Form 2. PLA   4   V   B   E   P

       V is the instrument number;

       B is the beginning beat of sound;

       E is the ending beat of sound;

       P is the initial value of all functions involved in the generation at beat B.

DUF — Specify duration and frequency line together

DUF   W   P   B(-3)   T(3)   O   F

Note that DUF constructs three functions, a FRE, a DUR, and a DTY function and numbers them F, F + 1, and F + 2, respectively.

SPT — Set parameter in third pass of MUSIC IV program

SPT   2   N   P

Parameter N is set to value P.

SPS — Set parameter in second pass of MUSIC IV

SPS   2   N   P

Parameter N is set to value P.

SPF — Set parameter in first pass of MUSIC IV

SPF   2   N   P

Parameter N is set to value P.

GEN — Generate a function in third pass of MUSIC IV

GEN   W P_1 P_2 P_3 ... P_{12}

This card works as any MUSIC IV parameter card with P_1 ... P_{12} being the parameters.

TER — Terminate composition

TER   1   1

PLS — Play a second-pass subroutine in MUSIC IV

PLS   W P_1 P_2 ... P_{12}

This card works exactly as any MUSIC IV parameter card with P_1 ... P_{12} being the parameters.

SEC — Terminate section

SEC   1   1

This card acts exactly as the SEC card in MUSIC IV.

CON — Continuation card

CON   W P_1 ... P_{12}

This card acts as an ETC card in MUSIC IV with $P_1 \ldots P_{12}$ being the standard parameters.

NUM — Set parameters in numerical memory

NUM   W   X $P_1 \ldots P_{12}$

This card acts as a NUM card in MUSIC IV with $P_1 \ldots P_{12}$ as the standard parameters and X, the function number in which the parameters are stored. Note that if $1 \leq X \leq 800$ the parameters are stored in pass I. If $X = 801$, the metronome function is stored in pass II (see MUSIC IV handbook[5]), and if $X > 801$ the parameters are stored in pass II.

III

Aesthetics

Rightness and wrongness are possible in regard to perception, and to perceive is to judge. While it is possible to judge rightly or wrongly, then in regard to perception as well rightness and wrongness must be possible.

ARISTOTLE: *Topica*, II.

Infraudibles

HERBERT BRÜN

University of Illinois
Urbana, Illinois

It is one thing to aim for a particular timbre of sound and then to search for the means of making such sound and timbre audible. It is another thing to provide for a series of events to happen and then to discover the timbre of the sounds so generated. In the first case one prefers those events to happen that one wishes to hear; in the second case one prefers to hear those events one wishes would happen. These are not only two different approaches to the composition of music but also two different political attitudes. As *Infraudibles* was produced according to this latter preference, I should like to see it understood as a piece of music that has some political significance to its musical idea and its process of composition.

By substituting sequences of different single periods for the modulation of simultaneous frequencies, the composer is able to control the infrastructures of the event, forming sounds just as precisely as the macro events of his composition. Thus "pitch" becomes a *result* of composition instead of functioning as an element. The same holds true for the concept of timbre. Still to be studied and evaluated are the differences between complex waveforms that are the result of instantaneous addition of amplitudes on the one hand and the results of the periodic repetition of sets containing sequences of different single periods on the other.

Even if it were true that the great masters of the past only rarely considered political and social issues as criteria that influenced their musical decision making in composition, this truth should not be trusted. The actual concern of composers for their contemporary environment is usually less known than suspected. By now many phenomena that until recently had been attributed to human frailty, to fate, or even to laws of nature have been recognized as issues of political and social rather than individual and natural significance. In any case, there is no historical proof that a composer remained uninfluenced by those issues that were of political or social importance in his day and environment, whether he knew it or not. All one is allowed to conjecture is that the less composers knew of this influence and the less they considered it, the more they became unconsciously dependent on it. To quote their words and writings usually only serves to show how dedicated they were to this state of being.

The most recent wave of growing awareness among artists and young people of the intrinsic unpleasantness that the systems we are caught in are pouring out over us with increasing generosity is an augmented version of the similar wave of 150 years ago. It should delight the protesting intellect to contemplate the possibility of an amalgamation between a twentieth-century romanticism and the pervading functional changes brought about internationally by the existence of high-speed electronic digital and analog computers. For it looks promising, almost reassuring, if for once an attempt is being made to couple the newest ideas for a better world with the latest knowledge about its potentials.

It is not surprising then that a few composers are beginning to look for answers to two questions:

1. Is it possible to incorporate the definition of a musical idea into a computer program so that this idea will generate the composition of its realization?

2. Is it possible to define a computer system and a computer program in which a musical idea functions as the generator of a system so structured that the sequence of its states could be called a "musical composition" by its composer?

The quest for answers to these questions has already produced a long line of audible experiments, some of which, having been undertaken by composers, demonstrate the distinct possibility of a musical solution to the problem set. Composers do not simply attempt to translate traditional techniques of composition into programming languages, nor are they interested in having the computer simulate conventional stilistic prejudices. They tend rather to start from scratch, to begin by stipulating what music is to be once the assistance of computers has become available. As a necessary preamble to this quite deliberate act of stipulation, it becomes incumbent on each composer to recall and understand that neither music nor computers grow wild in nature, that each of these concepts refers to systems created by humans, and that therefore it is obviously a new system, a system to be created, in which music and computers will mutually relate by analogy, by simulation, by structural correspondence, and by exploitation of one another's potential of information production, and consumption. The composer has to recall and understand that he is a rank beginner with the new system and that it were better if he achieved competence soon.

A particular system is defined by the number of elements it contains, by the number of states each of the elements can adopt, and by the number and kinds of algorithms that can function in this system, that can control the changes of state in this system, and provide the entrance to and the exit from the system. Such a definition refers only to the structure and thus to the information potential of a system. It neither implies the existence nor describes the nature of the elements. The definition actually reflects nothing but an image that someone chooses to give it, the image of that context in which, for him, a sequence of states or changes possesses relevance and significance. Systems are created by definitions. Definitions are created by people searching for relevance and significance in their own existence and in the existence of all or part of their environment. Without the concept of systems, the concepts of relevance and significance are meaningless. They are equally meaningless with regard to so-called "universal" or "natural" systems, in which everything is as it is and could not be otherwise because that is the way it is, "it" being everything. For anything to be of relevance to something, to be of significance to someone, a system has to be created; an artificially limited and conditioned system has to be imagined and then defined. Only artificial systems will clearly show that they have been elected by choice, thus implying the intended rejection of other, equally possible, yes, even equally reasonable systems. Everyone will agree that the quantity of possible or reasonable systems he could imagine far exceeds the number of those he may also call desirable. On the other hand, although few people would willingly support the statement that a system may just then be the most desirable when it appears most "impossible," most "unreasonable," this situation not only can be found often enough but actually suggests the present. Indeed all this clearly outlines the field of any relevant research in aesthetics.

Whether a stated concept corresponds to some truth can be verified by comparing its linguistic content with all linguistic contents in statements accepted as true. Whether a stated concept corresponds to some reality can be verified by comparing its linguistic contents with all linguistic contents in statements accepted as describing some reality. The objects of aesthetics, however, are statements not to be compared; unverifiable statements; statements corresponding to something wanting in existence. It is where truth as well as reality are in abeyance, but desire is not; there aesthetics sets up its deliberately stipulated values. If there is anything everlasting about aesthetics, it is the delightfully fascinating temporarity of its objects. It is on desires that aesthetics thrives and not on fulfilment. Here then is one valid connection between aesthetics and the arts. Just like aesthetics, the arts are more a statement of desire than of truth or reality, and just like aesthetics the arts develop an allergic sensitivity against all that is considered to be true or real. There should be no question of the desirability of all that is still neither real nor true, but desired above all. In contradiction to all religions, Eastern and Western, the arts and aesthetics condemn to obsolescence all that is believed to have been true always or to become true later. Instead they forcefully make their contemporaries aware of what might be real and true right now, regardless of recorded or predicted history.

Music, in its final appearance, as it arrives at the listener's ears, preserves at least traces of the processes by which it emerged from chaos. The composer, having to account for time, cannot entirely undo or replace it. As time is the inexorable accountant of sequences, either the cause or the result of events being looked at one after another, music is an analogy to all systems looked at in time, and just like all such systems irrelevant to time's past. This does not imply that the past is irrelevant to any system looked at in time. Relevance does not necessarily function both ways. No matter how much I admire the past, it simply cannot care about me and my acts; still, I have to acknowledge that the past not only has passed forever but that it also irreparably did happen. Thus the past belongs to truth and reality and not to the realm of desire. Music is stipulated not as time's victim but as time's employer. The composer of music is in a position to initiate an algorithm effectively in the system he creates that is analogous to the algorithm he would like to see initiated in the system that created him. The task of aesthetics, be it the composer's or the listener's, is to determine speculatively whether the analogy implies, at least structurally, events of contemporary relevance in the system called "environment" and whether the desires that motivated the composer to generate the musical process relate to desires motivating desirable processes in his contemporary society. It is not of primary importance for aesthetics whether everybody or even anybody agrees on the desirability of the processes implied by a work of art. This is rather the subject of political considerations. However, political considerations remain without tangible substance if the contemporary significance of individual acts and decisions is ignored and thus never properly evaluated. Any research of an aesthetical nature that fails to discover what, at a given time, is believed to be true and real and what, at the same time, is desired to be or become true and real instead fails to give food to political considerations and thus simply fails.

Example

Infraudibles
Side 4

This composition was produced with the assistance of several computer programs. The "score" was generated by a FORTRAN program written by the author for the IBM 7094 and was used as input (via digital magnetic tape) to a sound-generator program written by Gary Grossman for the Illiac II computer.

A unique method for producing complex timbres was used throughout the piece. Segments of sine waves of different frequencies were joined together to produce a complex waveform. Although the result in theory is a periodic waveform, the audible effect resembles clusters of inharmonic frequencies, since frequencies of relatively prime partials can be accentuated in this manner. Automatic segment joining and pitch changing was accomplished by a special MACRO facility of Grossman's program.

Waveform samples were computed and converted to analog form by using the Illiac II analog-digital facility.

Operations on Wave Forms*

J. K. RANDALL

Princeton University
Princeton, New Jersey

However useful the concept of "timbre" may be for music in which relations of spectrum, vibrato, tremolo, and so forth, are less elaborately
structured compositionally than are relations of pitch and rhythm, new
possibilities for articulating musical structure (that have arisen specifically by virtue of the control given us, by electronic media, over each "in-
gredient" of timbre separately) are rendering this concept, if not useless,
then at least misleading and inhibiting both to current research and to
current composition. If we contend, for example, that vibrato is a component of timbre; and that to exert beneficent influence upon a timbre, a
vibrato must be moderate in speed (say, several cycles per second, not
several per minute or several hundred per second) and well within the
boundary of the chromatic semi-tone in width, with both speed and
width of course somewhat randomized; then we must recognize that
such contentions invoke, at least tacitly, our generalized remembrance of
what vibrato "sounds like" (or, worse, *ought to* "sound like") in familiar
musical contexts—that is, in contexts where vibrato is not among the
most highly compositionally structured aspects of sound. I am concerned
here not with the demonstrable [1] irrelevance of this generalized remembrance even to those contexts which our remembrance generalizes
upon; I am concerned here rather with the musically useful results of
considering, say, vibrato as a perceivable, structurable, and electronically
controllable musical continuum in its own right: that is, with perceptions
which only the music of the future and the very recent past can induce us
to make. Please keep in mind that such refinement and extension of our

---

*This article is Lecture III from "Three Lectures to Scientists," reprinted with permission
of the author and publishers from *Perspectives of New Music,* Vol. 5, No. 2, Princeton
University Press, Princeton, N. J. (1967), pp. 134–140.

abilities to perceive, and more importantly of the very modes in which we perceive, is one of the more basic and traditional roles of the art of music.

In compositionally exploiting vibrato as such a continuum, let's consider what it would initially seem reasonable to *avoid*. First, I would recommend avoiding techniques which reduce vibrato to the least structurally relevant of its traditional roles: namely, the role of subliminally "lushing-up" tone quality. Second, I would avoid segmenting my continuum on the model of generalized remembrance: identifying a particular segment as the good stuff or the real thing and everything outside that segment as "too" this or "too" that can only stultify my compositional imagination at the outset, and thereby prevent me from ever inducing those very perceptions I ought to be most solicitous about. Instead, I would simply ask myself in moving along this continuum: what kind of musical structures can I imagine that would most strikingly exploit, and thereby make most perceptible to me, the relations I think I ought to be able to hear? My most interesting problems will arise not where I think "normal" passes over into abnormal vibrato; but rather where vibrato itself seems to pass over, first, from a wiggling *of* pitch into some sort of noise *around* a pitch, and then over into a complex mode of pitch-*production* in which the center frequency, the speed of the vibrato, the difference between the two, the sum of the two, the frequencies which delimit the width of the vibrato, and individual frequencies of the spectrum to which the vibrato is applied, all participate as principal components. And these problems will not necessarily be "resolved" by my determining, democratically or otherwise, just where within my continuum each boundary lies — rather, I would expect that, just as the right musical context could fully articulate, for my perception, one of these boundaries, so some other musical context could either dissolve that boundary or reduce to contextual irrelevance the very terms in which it was defined. In short, these seeming boundaries might well prove to be musical structural relations internal to and dependent upon specific musical contexts — and not psycho-acoustical "facts" about the "materials" of music. And third, I would avoid saturating individual tones with additional, contextually nonsignificant, ingredients, chosen to instrumentalize, i.e., lush-up, electronically generated timbres. Instead, I would devote my attention to musically developing however few or many timbral ingredients a compositional idea may suggest in somewhat the sense that I would try to musically develop basic configurations of pitch and rhythm. The often-deplored uniformity, monotony, or outright nastiness of electronic timbres seems to me more properly analyzed as a failure of some existing electronic compositions adequately to structure and develop their timbral components as elements of the composition, rather than as any inherent debility in current technology or any musical dullness "inherent" even in the balder electronic timbres. It is of course simply true that we can produce an electronic tone each of whose components remains uniform from the beginning of the tone to the end; and that a composition which spends 15 or 20 minutes, or even 1 or 2 minutes, celebrating this truth courts triviality. But a composition which meets the threat of triviality with a barrage of irrelevancies is at least as feeble a composition; and perhaps a feebler one, in that it explicitly presents so many things which—specifically by virtue of electronics—could have been musically developed. If I am willing, in instrumental music, to put up with that hopefully rather small percentage of the total sound which *can't* fairly be said to participate constructively in any "local open-ended agglomeration of musical developments in progress"—that is, with these musical irrelevancies which lush-up the tone—this is no reason why I should be willing to put up with them in electronic music where we have become for the first time free to build into individual tones precisely what the musical contexts may suggest *and no more;* that is, free to treat the individual tone as something which need resemble in no degree whatever an extra-structurally prefilled garbage-can.

Now vibrato is just one of the many potentially structurable aspects of sound which have been too often, in effect, written off as ingredients of something more vague. I would like to discuss specifically a few of the characteristics of sets of partials, harmonic and nonharmonic, which composers including myself have tried to release from subliminal influence upon the "timbre," and to develop musically as compositional elements.

In the right musical context, it becomes quite easy to perceive and relate sets of partials in the following terms:

1. Registral position: that is, position of any set in the pitch continuum—regardless of the pitches of perceived or unperceived "fundamentals."
2. Intervallic spread: that is, the musical interval defined by the highest and lowest frequencies in any set.
3. Density: that is, the average number of elements in a set which lie within some relevant standard musical interval.
4. Total number of elements in a set.
5. The distribution of relative amplitude over any set.
6. Physical place or places from which any set, or any element of a set, seems to emanate.

This list could obviously be extended; but it is already sufficiently detailed to provide a basis for defining some musical operations on sets of partials—operations many of which may be viewed as attempts to capitalize upon the capacities of electronic media in order to subject to elaborate and continuous musical structuring aspects of sound which the composer for instrumental media cannot risk reliance upon except for rather gross general contrasts and rather subtle local articulations. For example, we know that certain instruments can noticeably transform their tone-qualities in the course of single notes: strings, say, by sliding and tilting the bow; winds, say, by slowly inserting or removing a mute. We know that, in percussion instruments especially, different components of the spectrum fade out at different rates; that most instruments have some junk in the attack; that the component partials, even during "steady state," fluctuate in amplitude; that many instruments can, in a highly limited degree, vary their speeds and widths of vibrato and amplitude modulation; that certain percussion instruments produce sounds which lie in a tantalizing no-man's-land between definite and indefinite pitch; and that the physical positions of several instruments relative to one another can be of structural musical, as well as of acoustical, consequence. But because of the severe limitations imposed upon the compositional exploitation of all these facts of instrumental sound by the physical limitations of instruments and the human body, it is computers, and not conventional instruments, that have the capacity to really capitalize even upon instrumentally-suggested transformations of waveform,* whether over the course of a whole composition, from note to note, or within single notes. Partly in this connection I have welcomed the chance offered by computers to try using exclusively sets of partials (harmonic and nonharmonic) derived from one another and pitchconfigurations basic to a composition by operations appropriate to that composition; and certain operations have been sufficiently appropriate to a composition I am now working on for me to have incorporated them as alternative branches in a Music IV subroutine. These operations upon sets of partials, in the use of which I lean heavily on the assumption that in the right musical context we can perceive the characteristics I have listed, are the following:

1. Mappings of basic sets of partials onto enlarged and compressed spaces:

(My subroutine does this by preserving the proportions among the component musical intervals of the basic set of partials while gradually changing the intervals themselves. In the continuum thus generated, the basic set itself corresponds to the point of zero enlargement of the total space.)

---

*I ask the reader's indulgence for my continuing to include physical places of origin among the "properties" of a waveform and hence among its transformables.

2. Mappings of basic sets which preserve frequency differences while gradually changing the musical intervals:

(My subroutine does this by adding a constant to each of the partial numbers. In the continuum thus generated, the basic set itself corresponds to the constant zero. I should perhaps here emphasize that the relation between a set of partial-numbers and its corresponding musical intervals and the relation between a set of frequency-numbers and its corresponding musical intervals is one and the same relation: specifically, a given ratio, whether of partial-numbers or frequency-numbers, corresponds to the same musical interval. Hence my subroutine—whose variable arguments are largely operation-codes and musical intervals—treats partial-numbers with impunity as if they were, in effect, frequency numbers.)

3. Mappings of basic sets which exponentiate the partial-numbers by a constant:

(In the continuum thus generated, the basic set itself corresponds to the constant *one*. Since it is not intuitively obvious to me what the musical intervallic result might be of exponentiating partial-numbers by, say, the constant 3.508, the relevant variable argument for this (as for any other) operation in my subroutine is a desired intervallic spread of the result: the subroutine computes whatever mysterious constant it needs to get that intervallic result.)

4. Mappings of basic sets which treat partial-numbers themselves as exponents for a constant base:

(This operation is suggested by the rather well known effects of using the twelfth-root of two as a base for integral exponents. However, it should be noticed that this operation has one characteristic which fundamentally distinguishes it from the other operations I have discussed: in the continuum thus generated, the basic set itself does not in general appear at all.)

5. Mappings of basic sets onto their total inversions—intervallic, frequency-differential, or exponential.

(In order to retrieve for me my control over the assorted registral positions of the assorted new spectra generated by sequences and combinations of these operations applied to derived as well as to basic sets of partials, my subroutine accepts a transposition-number as one of its variable arguments: for example, any derived set at transposition zero will have the same weighted center as the set from which it was derived. I hope it is clear without illustration that, because of the sheer messiness of the calculations required, the computer is as necessary in deriving the new sets of partials in the first place as it is in simulating soundwaves resulting from their use. And yet the results of appropriate musical use of these operations seem to me quite readily perceivable as various kinds and degrees of intervallic distortion, while quite distinguishable in musical function from "chords.")*

In compositionally using any such derivations as these, we now have, realistically, the chance to structure developments within any single note exclusively in ways that reflect developments, or the principles of development, in a composition as a whole. There is no longer any gross physical limitation upon the particular ways in which, during a single note, one set of partials may become transformed into another; upon the particular rhythms in which structurally relevant chunks of a total spectrum may fade out — whether immediately following the attack or more gradually during an eminently unsteady state; upon the relevant permutations of amplitude-values which any single set of partials occupying an entire note may undergo; upon the range over which speeds and widths of vibrato and amplitude modulation may change during a single note; upon particular ways in which a single note may fluctuate between definite and indefinite pitch; or upon the complexity of arrangement of moving and stationary sources from which various stereophonic sounds seem to emanate.

If I have repeatedly directed my discussion from electronic possibilities in general toward possibilities for single tones in particular, it is in order to suggest a realistic alternative to the stultifying concept of "timbre": I think that concern with electronic "timbre" should be replaced by, and indeed probably has as its only salvageable inspiration, the compositional exploration of modes of musical development within single tones. The new electronic possibilities may even lead us to the belief that the concept of "timbre" was really never much more than the repository of some notion that individual tones have "moods." We long ago quit talking about "happy melodies" and "pungent harmonies" in favor of contextual musical analysis of developing musical structures of, primarily, pitch and rhythm; and I would hope that we could soon find

---

*Notice the injustice of claiming any more radical distinction between sets of partials and sets of simultaneous notes (i.e., "chords") in the case, say, of an orchestral performance of a Mozart symphony: it's not that we *can't* hear those individual overtones *if we try:* on the contrary, it's by succeeding in the attempt that we most convincingly reinforce our musically well-founded determination *not* to. Somehow our musical intelligence persuades us to absorb these overtones as qualifications of fundamentals; much as it persuades us to absorb an assortment of messages traceable to balky (plastic) gut, slithering (plastic) horsehair, dental protruberance, and salivary dispersion as qualifications of attack. In these cases as normally, our ears admirably perceive in modes conducive to musical sense.

whatever further excuse we still need to quit talking about "mellow timbres" and "edgy timbres," and "timbres" altogether, in favor of contextual musical analysis of developing structures of vibrato, tremolo, spectral transformation, and all those various dimensions of sound which need no longer languish as inmates of some metaphor.

REFERENCE

[1] J. K. Randall, "New Sounds" vs. Musical Articulation, Lecture II in "Three Lectures to Scientists," *Perspectives of New Music,* Vol. 5, No. 2, (Princeton University Press, 1967), pp. 130–134.

Example

Variation 6-10 (1966)
by J. K. Randall
Side 1

In realizing this composition, the Princeton University IBM 7094 computer was used for computing the waveform samples with Max Mathews' Music IV program and the Bell Laboratories digital/analog facility was used to convert the samples into an audible signal.

Control of Consonance and Dissonance with Nonharmonic Overtones

J. R. PIERCE AND M. V. MATHEWS

Bell Telephone Laboratories
Murray Hill, New Jersey

One of us has already pointed out the possibility of attaining consonance in strange scales by using nonharmonic overtones or partials [1]. This article reviews the earlier argument and describes some further work.

Following the proposal of Helmholtz, Plomp and Levelt assert that two sinusoidal tones are consonant either if their frequencies coincide or if they are sufficiently separated. Thus complex tones with harmonic partials will be consonant when the frequencies of their fundamentals bear certain simple numerical ratios. Further, Plomp and Levelt [2] give a quantitative prescription for the separation of those partials necessary for consonance. On the basis of psychoacoustical experiments they present a curve that expresses degree of consonance as a function of separation as a fraction of the critical bandwidth.

Tones are most dissonant when their frequencies are separated by a particular fraction of a critical bandwidth and are consonant when their frequencies coincide or are separated by more than a critical bandwidth. Using this idealized curve, Plomp and Levelt calculate the consonance for various ratios of frequencies. This computed consonance is greatest at certain peaks which occur at ratios of frequencies for traditionally consonant intervals. The experimental curves from which Plomp and Levelt derive these idealized curves correspond roughly with them but perhaps favor somewhat the consonance of the octave.

If we accept the results of Plomp and Levelt, there is a simple explanation for the rather unpleasant quality of many electronic tones which have a large number of harmonics. The higher harmonics are simply too close together, measured in terms of the critical bandwidth, and this gives rise to dissonance, which could also be described as having a buzzy

quality; for instance, if we listen to a tone with 10 harmonic partials*
ranging from 200 to 2000 Hz, we find it buzzy or perhaps lacking consonance. However, a tone with five octave partials ranging from 2000 to
3200 Hz is richer than a simple sinusoidal tone but has none of the mechanical, buzzy, or dissonant qualities of the tone with 10 harmonic partials. A tone with eight octaves and fifths, ranging from 200 to 2400 Hz
also has a pleasing and rather nonmechanical quality. A tone with 11 octaves, major thirds, and fifths ranging from 200 to 2000 Hz is also pleasing. A tone with 11 octaves, major thirds, and minor sixths ranging from
200 to 2000 Hz seems a little less smooth than octaves, major thirds, and
fifths.

We think it is clear that tones with partials that are not crowded too
closely together at high frequencies can be pleasing or consonant. A tone
with octave partials certainly is. But need the partials be exactly octave
partials? If we were guided merely by the conclusions of Plomp and Levelt, we would feel that making the partials almost octave partials should
be just as good. We compared a tone consisting of five octave partials
ranging from 200 to 2000 Hz with a tone consisting of five partials given
by 2.1 to the nth power (octave partials would be given by 2 to the nth
power). These not-quite-octave partials range from 200 to 3713 Hz.
There was a clear difference in quality. The tone of the almost-octave
partials did not have the smoothness of the tone with octave partials.
Thus, in a practical way, there seems to be something sacred about the
octave. We can say, if we wish, that this has to do with the phase relations
among the partials, or we can believe that the unpleasant effects of the
almost-octave partials arise through sum and difference frequencies of
various complicated sorts falling near to some of the sinusoidal components of the tone. Whatever the explanation may be, partials separated
by exact octaves have a quite different effect from partials separated by
approximate octaves, even though the partials are several critical bandwidths apart.

Although the octave appears to be an important interval in terms of
tone quality, this may not necessarily be so for other musical intervals. A
tone whose partials are successively a half-octave apart (by a half-octave
we mean a frequency ratio of $\sqrt{2}$) and range from 200 to 3200 Hz was
compared with a tone in which the partials use either octaves or are a
fifth removed from octaves. This tone again had partials in the range 200
to 3200 Hz. The intervals between partials in the first tone were the tritone, a diminished fifth or augmented fourth, which is generally considered to be dissonant. Although the first tone was perhaps a little less
smooth than the second, we found it was easy to regard both as musical
in quality.

*In all experiments the partials went down in amplitude 9 DB per octave.

Thoughts along these lines led us to explore tones in which the partials were separated by various fractions of an octave. In these tones some of the partials were octave partials but others were separated from the fundamental or its octaves by various small fractions of the musical octave. We listened successively to tones with five octave partials, nine one-half octave partials, 12 one-quarter octave partials, and 17 one-eighth octave partials. To our ears, as the tones became somewhat fuller or richer as the partials were put closer together, the tone with quarter-octave partials could still be considered as consonant, whereas the tone whose partials differed by an eighth of an octave was clearly dissonant or noisy.

As a kind of distraction from considerations of telephone transmission and speech quality, and phenomena that may be important to them, one of us was led to speculate on the utility of tones with nonharmonic partials in musical composition. To this end he composed a four-voice canon in a scale in which the octave is divided into eight equal intervals (Figure 1). Each voice starts out as a sinusoidal tone, then becomes a tone with octave partials, a tone with half-octave partials, and a tone with quarter-octave partials; the number of partials is then reduced to two per octave and one per octave, and finally we have at last a sinusoidal tone.

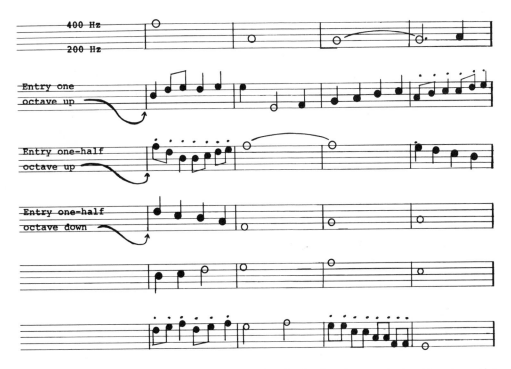

Figure 1. *Eight Tone Canon* by J. R. Pierce. Each voice is played successively with a sinusoidal wave form, then with partials spaced an octave apart, then a half-octave apart, then a quarter of an octave apart, and so on back to a sinusoid.

In some bars of this canon the voices have no frequencies closer than a quarter of an octave for any of the tone qualities used. In other bars of the canon the voices may contain partials an eighth of an octave apart, which we have just heard to be dissonant. Thus we expect — and we hear — a sort of dissonance, especially toward the middle of the canon, in which all the tones have partials only a quarter of an octave apart.

We wish to thank J. Kohut for synthesizing the tones we have referred to.

REFERENCES

[1] J. R. Pierce, Attaining Consonance in Arbitrary Scales, *J. Acoust. Soc. Am.*, **40**, 249 (1966).

[2] R. Plomp and W. J. M. Levelt, Tonal Consonance and Critical Bandwidth, *J. Acoust. Soc. Am.*, **38**, 548–560 (1965).

Example

Eight Tone Canon
by J. R. Pierce, August 17, 1966
Side 6, Band 2

This is a four-voice cannon in a scale in which the octave is divided into eight equal intervals. Each voice, starting out as a sine wave, progressively changes into a tone with octave, half-octave, and finally quarter-octave partials, whereupon the numbers of partials are reduced in the reverse fashion so that a sine tone again remains. The result is that certain portions of the composition contain frequencies no closer than a quarter-octave, whereas in other portions the frequencies of the voices are as close as an eighth-octave. The concept of "voice" really breaks down here. This provides a control on dissonance, which is assumed to increase inversely with the difference between frequencies. The dissonance climax was designed to be at the middle of the canon, where all tones have partials only a quarter-octave apart.

The Problem of Imperfection in Computer Music

GERALD STRANG

California State College at Long Beach
Long Beach, California

"Sound" signifies different concepts to those concerned with audible vibrations from various viewpoints. To the physicist or the acoustician it signifies the audible product of a vibrating body or the conditions it produces in a transmitting medium. To the psychologist it refers to sensations in the ear or the perception that results from such sensations. To the performer of music it is the sensation complicated by an elaborate body of conventions and traditions that produce value judgments. To the composer it is all these and an expressive medium as well. From any musical point of view sound must be considered (at the simplest) as a physical phenomenon that produces sensations subject to interpretation and evaluation based on esthetic criteria.

Theoretical and experimental analysis of sound has produced a variety of generalizations and assumptions alleged to explain at least its physical nature and behavior but which are by no means mutually consistent. Many are based on study of an instantaneous sample or an isolated phenomenon of short duration. Others deal with limited aspects of complex conditions. The complexity of musical sound over a significant period breeds either analytical oversimplification or statistical generality.

Early attempts at electronic sound synthesis assumed that equivalents of natural acoustical sounds could be created by reversing the analytical process.

The timbre of a steady sound can be subjected to Fourier analysis and represented as a sum of sine waves. The formant theory helps to explain the relationship of timbres which vary with the pitch of the fundamental. Attack and decay characteristics can be analyzed in terms of transients and envelope contours.

The engineer, in designing equipment for electronic sound synthesis, creates a model that simplifies and generalizes the fragmentary theories derived from such analyses. Fourier synthesis may be attempted by combining batteries of oscillators. Filters may contribute formants, or they may be used to shape abstract waveforms (sine, square, pulse, sawtooth). Envelope generators may control attack and decay rates. However complex the system, it consists of units, each of which behaves as regularly, consistently, and predictably as possible.

Thus synthesized sound is inherently simpler and more regular than natural acoustical sound. If this is true of analog sound, it tends to be even truer of computer synthesis. The mathematical model further regularizes the already oversimplified engineering model.

Sound is a vibratory phenomenon. Simple oscillations are periodic. In the earlier literature a distinction was made between musical sound (periodic, regular) and noise (aperiodic, erratic). *Periodicity* is, then, a basic assumption. Even noise is often described as if it were a mixture of periodic wave trains covering a wide frequency range or a series of oscillations at randomly changing frequencies, the rate of change being too rapid for the ear to distinguish. Thus the *aperiodic* is treated as a special case of the *periodic*.

In musical sound, considered over any reasonable length of time, periodicity in the exact sense appears to be illusory. Some parameters maintain periodicity more precisely than others but even pitch tends to drift slightly or to be modulated by a pitch vibrato which itself is not quite periodic. *Quasiperiodicity* would be a better term for application to music of the past.

Electronic and computer synthesis depends heavily on the establishment of a single-cycle waveform, which is then repeated with great precision at whatever frequency will produce the desired pitch. Whatever the basic waveform, the goal is a *perfect repetition*.

Digitizing for computer sound synthesis depends in the most fundamental way on absolute regularity and periodicity. A small difference in the sampling rate from run to run may not cause difficulty, but within a given run the digital data must be supplied to the digital-to-analog converter at a rate controlled with utmost precision.

The goal of perfect periodicity is applied at other levels. An envelope (attack and decay pattern) is normally fixed by setting certain time constants, or at best it becomes a low-level dependent variable, proportionate, perhaps, to the length of the note. Successions of events occur at rigorously fixed rates or perhaps at rates that change in a simple, readily recognized way.

Even the repetition of musical ideas, of melodic or rhythmic patterns, tends to be obviously predictable. If variations are introduced, they tend to be repetitive, regular, or at best permutative.

From the esthetic viewpoint simple periodicity controlled by elementary arithmetical manipulations becomes intolerable about as soon as the listener becomes aware of the system. Schoenberg attributed to Beethoven the aphorism: "Everything in music must be at once surprising and expected." If this is valid, the artist must continuously balance the *determinate* against the *indeterminate;* the *anticipated* against the *unanticipated.*

Quasiperiodicity (at least while listeners are evaluating experimental music in terms of criteria acquired from traditional sound-generating media) appears to offer greater esthetic potential than the regimentation characteristic of computer operations.

It is not clear whether the apparent human preference for the imprecise, the unpredictable, in art is due to human inability to achieve perfect precision. We may be rationalizing human frailty. Nevertheless, it seems probable that at this point in the history of musical taste the perfect periodicity of theory and the perfect repetition natural to computers must be modified in the interest of esthetic acceptability.

How can we introduce appropriate *imperfection in computer music?* At what levels and by what means?

The unanticipated can be introduced by the composer in the grosser aspects of composition. He can control melodic, harmonic, and formal variation as in conventional composition. He can also create patterns so long and complex that repetitions are difficult to recognize. He can contrive aperiodic dislocations of periodic events à la Stravinsky. He can perhaps invent algorithms to modify algorithms. He can, following Hiller, substitute probabilities for certainties. He can introduce random elements within carefully controlled limits.

In the synthesis of the sound itself the number of events precludes direct control of the details. The computer must be programmed to introduce the irregularities.

It appears unlikely that irregularity in the sampling rate would be meaningful or practicable (though there are some interesting implications). At higher levels both systematic and random variations may be used to break down exact periodicity.

The remainder of this article describes some experiments made at UCLA with a version of the Bell Telephone Laboratories MUSIC IV program, rewritten in FORTRAN IV and MAP and executed on an IBM 7094 computer.

TIMBRE

The most economical way to produce computer sound is to store a single cycle of each waveform having the desired tone quality. Any pitch may then be produced by scanning the stored function at a rate that causes it to be repeated at the desired frequency. Thus 440 repetitions of the waveform per second will be heard as "Violin A."

Each cycle (within the limits of accuracy of the scanning process) is a duplicate of any other. The waveform remains the same at any frequency. Normally the algebraic sum of all components reaches an amplitude of zero at the beginning and end of each cycle. This is a "frozen function."

The complex sound of a musical instrument owes some of its warmth, variety, and interest to continuous interaction among its components. Phase relations between fundamental and overtones may shift. Inharmonic overtones may cause a continuous change in the composite waveform. The relative amplitudes of elements may change during the life of the tone. This kind of continuously changing sound cannot be achieved by the simple repetition of a single stored function.

The attempt to introduce inharmonic overtones by using nonintegral multipliers in Fourier synthesis does not achieve the desired flexibility. The single stored cycle does not reach an identical value at its beginning and end. Thus a discontinuity occurs at the beginning of each cycle, with attendant transient distortion. This may add an interesting "bite," but in more extreme cases a rough, penetrating noise covers the desired timbre (see Examples 4 and 5).

Continuous generation of a complex containing inharmonic overtones can produce fascinating sounds, but it is incredibly expensive in computer time. It requires what amounts to a bank of oscillators, each contributing its increment to each composite sample. Example 1 demonstrates such a sound at a number of different pitches.* Three minutes of computer time were required to calculate one second of sound—a 180:1 time scale!

Clearly more efficient ways of securing such continuously varying sounds need to be devised.

VIBRATO

Vibrato is a complicated method of quasiperiodic modulation of an otherwise monotonous periodic wave train. As used in live performance, it involves modulation of pitch, amplitude, and sometimes timbre. Even the rate varies within narrow limits.

---

*This example was programmed by Dr. John Gardner and is based on an investigation of nonharmonic ratios based on powers of e, carried out by Professor Leon Knopoff.

Example 2 uses a pitch vibrato only. It is basically the modulation of a complex wave train with an 8-Hz sine wave. Bandwidths are 1 and 2% of the pitch frequency. The eight-cycle rate is then progressively modified by random variation within the limits: 7 to 9 Hz; 6 to 10 Hz; 5 to 11 Hz. The final example is 1% at a rate varying randomly between 9 and 11 Hz.

Some of these are intolerable to musicians; others are reasonably acceptable. To simulate a natural vibrato would require more controls. Both frequency and amplitude tend to change progressively during the note. Under some conditions the vibrato grows in width and rate after the attack. In other cases it may be reduced near the end.

There is some indication that the vibrato need not be so complex in electronic music and that a narrower faster vibrato is desirable than would be used by a violinist.

PITCH REPETITION

The monotony of repetition suggests that small random variations of pitch might be helpful. Example 3 illustrates (a) simple repetition, (b) random pitch variation increasing from $\frac{1}{2}$ to 2%, and (c) random pitch variation decreasing from 1 to 0%.

The ear appears to tolerate this kind of pitch variation less well than the vibrato type. A systematic vibrato that varies the pitch within a band equal to $f + 1\%$ seems wide, but it is not unreasonable. The pitch is heard as being essentially stable. Repeated notes within the same band are heard as different pitches.

ENVELOPE

Several of the "instruments" used in Examples 4 and 5 introduce a selection process, the envelope being chosen according to the duration of the note from four stored alternatives. Under some conditions a larger number of alternatives would be desirable, and the choice should depend on additional factors such as pitch and amplitude. The listener probably cannot detect the alternatives because they all have similar contours.

RATE CHANGES

Metrical regularity can also be heard as excessively dry. Small random temporal shifts, or rate changes, seemed worth investigating. To illustrate them in combination with some of the other methods described two short pieces were composed.

Pitches are specified (in just intonation) in one voice but in another are random within specified limits. Some of the timbres are fuzzy or harsh because of the introduction of inharmonic partials which produce discontinuities from cycle to cycle.

In each case the first version is "straight"—no attempt is made to disguise regularity in any parameter. In successive repetitions vibrato, rates, pitches and amplitudes are made subject to progressive variation:

Example 4: Score #5, Orch. #15—three versions
Example 5: Score x, Orch. #13—two versions

CONCLUSIONS

Only the most tentative conclusions can be drawn. The experiments should be amplified and broadened to explore these factors in more detail. Degree of variation of each parameter is critical. Random modulation is evidently not the answer in some cases, though it seems useful in others. The value of small interruptions or shifts—the dislocation of periodic repetition—should be investigated. Slowly changing systematic modification is another possibility.

Only the opinions of listeners can evaluate these factors. Limited opinion sampling, with both experienced and inexperienced listeners, indicates that professional performers prefer a higher level of regularity and accuracy than nonperformers. Neither type appears to approve of the maximum level of computer "perfection." Listeners object to the "electronic organ sound" or the "machine sound" and ask for more warmth or spontaneity.

Even if extensive opinion sampling were carried out, we would know only what listeners think now, based on conventional literature in conventional performance. There is no reason to believe that such judgments will remain unchanged after listeners have been exposed to much more synthetic sound. Perhaps they prefer "imperfection" primarily because they have never heard anything else.

EXAMPLES

Inharmonic Partials
Side 7, Band 1

Vibrato
Side 7, Band 2

Pitch Fluctuations
Side 7, Band 3

Score 5, Orchestra No. 15
Side 7, Band 4

1. Without fluctuations
2. Regular vibrato; changing rates
3. Varying vibrato; wider variation of rates

Score X, Orchestra No. 13
Side 7, Band 5

1. Without fluctuations
2. Random variations of pitch and rate

The examples were realized with the UCLA IBM 7094 digital-analog conversion facility making use of the Music IV program.

Author
first/name
not on barcode